Reverend George Graham Price
whose spiritual name
was Frater Achad

Ancient Mystical White Brotherhood

Frater Achad
Spiritual Name
of
Reverend George Graham Price

Great Seal Press Publisher

Copyright © 1971
Revised fourth edition 1991
Copyright © 1991 Constance Rogge

For further information, write to:
GREAT SEAL PRESS PUBLISHER
P.O. Box 10771
Phoenix, AZ 85064

Printed in the United States of America

Publisher's Cataloging in Publication
(Prepared by Quality Books, Inc.)

Price, George Graham, 1889-1959
    Ancient Mysical White Brotherhood — Frater Achad. — p. cm.
    ISBN 0-926872-02-8
    1. Ancient Mystical White Brotherhood. 2. Channeling (Spiritualism)
    3. Melchizedek, King of Salem. 4. Bible — Criticism, interpretation, etc.
    I. Title.

BF1311.A53P7 1990   133.91

                                              QBI90-60
                                              MARC

ISBN: 0-926872-02-8

TABLE OF CONTENTS

PREFACE

This book is prepared with a sacred reverence to the great spiritual teachers who have preceded us in life on Earth and whose endless task is to point to the base of reference for mankind, to which he must become oriented. The instructions and guidance from these great ones is always given in a simple, direct manner; it is never necessary to resort to dictionaries or encyclopedias in order to fully grasp the spiritual value.

No attempt is made to conform to artificial literary standards nor to any world authority. The masters never use involved intellectual terminology, regardless of any human opinion, for the nearer one comes to the eternal truth, the more direct and concise is the terminology.

In the Congressional Library in Washington, D.C., there is an inscription over one of the doorways, "Man is in one world and hath another to attend him." This blessing, this grace of God which sustains us all is a proof of the validity of the material in this book, i.e., the brotherhood of man under the Fatherhood of God, and the ceaseless effort of those unknown great ones who are unseen to human eyes. What have we done to merit this?

At no time has man been without guidance to a life that is in harmony with the Infinite. However, it has always been man's responsibility to render himself receptive to that guidance through the cultivation of purity, humility and love.

The chapters of this book represent a record of such guidance which has come to certain individuals who were sincerely seeking it, not for self alone, but to share that knowledge. The relationship which is reflected throughout the chapters and the conversational tones to the messages, the unique individuality, is explicit and to the point, while they impart universal and impersonal truth.

How the messages were received is not important. The merely curious will be disappointed, for no attempt is made to gratify the dilettante or curiosity seeker. Sincere students of the mysteries of life understand that truth needs no other confirmation than the joyful response of one's own heart.

They will be encouraged to hold fast to what they have already found, to persevere in their aspirations. They will pay heed to the frequent and repeated admonitions, which are very important if one is to grow in love and reverence. We found that certain key principles and laws were repeated over and over again, to drive the essential point to the mark. This might have been because they were aware, by the light of our auras, that the fullness of what was related to us was not being fully grasped. Therefore they repeated it again and again, to clarify as "unto babes, young in soul growth," thus to lead to the enlargement of our understanding, enabling man to cooperate with these immutable laws that govern the universe in which man was captive, yet possessed "free will." We trust this repetition will be accepted in love, as it is intended.

We trust that even the stranger to the ways of spirit will also benefit from the thoughtful reading of this book and will come to realize that in the more vital aspects of human existence, authenticity is a matter of spiritual perception and that the quality of the product bears witness to its source. Such contemplation may lead him to the new meaning of Shakespeare's observation that, "There are more things in heaven and Earth than are dreamed of in your philosophy."

The meaning of these principles unfolds in greater depth, as we learn the lessons life provides, and brings blessings to each according to his needs and the sincerity of his application to problems, which will make us and not break us.

With deep, warm-hearted gratitude, I wish to thank my many dear friends who have given me the encouragement and assistance to do the compilation of materials to present it to the readers, that they too might be blessed in the reading of it, as it has blessed those who have already come in contact with the information the great ones meant for all whom they are calling now.

"Unto thee I grant ... so be it."

Natasha Greenlee

BIOGRAPHY OF
REVEREND GEORGE GRAHAM PRICE
whose spiritual name was Frater Achad

Reverend George G. Price came into our lives in
the early fall of 1953, after a senior couple from Gary,
Indiana, Natasha and George Greenlee, recently mar-
ried, had spent most of two years traveling across the
country looking for a truly high quality metaphysical
teacher. There were a number of fine men available
publicly, but for some indefinite reason, none were
quite who or what they seemed to be searching for.

A friend announced over dinner, "Dear, I've just
heard of the perfect teacher for you. His name is — oh,
heck, I promised that I wouldn't tell anyone about
him. He has retired completely from the public. I
guess I shouldn't have mentioned him." However,

before the evening was over, Mrs. Greenlee had the teacher's name and telephone number safely in her purse.

A few days later, the Greenlee's decided to call the teacher to make an appointment. The response was that he had withdrawn from the public permanently. When they asked about access to his wonderful philosophy, of which they'd heard, he replied that he had a student who had public classes in the subject at the South Bend YMCA, Sunday mornings and Thursday evenings, to which they would be most welcome.

Thursday evening found them at the appointed place a half an hour early, waiting expectantly. Mrs. Greenlee fretted, "What will I say when he asks who told us of them? I promised Ruth not to reveal her identity." Her husband calmly said, "Just leave it to me."

Finally the elevator stopped at that floor and an elderly, stooped gentlemen walked out with a young, vibrant, red-haired man. Suddenly, a voice called out, "How did you find us? We had despaired of ever seeing you."

The couple looked up and down the hall. There was still only the four there. They asked, "Who do you mean, us?" as the gentlemen approached and replied, "Yes, of course. You two."

The Greenlee couple introduced themselves to the teacher, Rev. George Graham Price, and his student, Eugene Lockhart. When asked again, "How did you find us? Who told you where we were?", Mr. Greenlee looked them sternly in the eye, replying, "If you can't tell us that, you aren't what we are looking for, and you'll never see us again." The laughing reply was, "I see the name Ruth ——————— in an arch over your heads." (It was the name of the woman friend).

That reply was the least remarkable of the accomplishments of Rev. Price which we were to enjoy in the following six years of his life. Gene, it developed later, was seriously ill with diabetes. He, too, was a fountain of wonderful information, but he had an uncontrollable sweet tooth and serious diabetes that, at that time, was not easily medicated. He only lived a couple of years more.

They both soon moved into the Greenlee home and the wonderful lessons that came through George Price quickly attracted a fascinating and loyal group.

While he was a highly educated and well-read man — and we got to know him personally very well — most of the material which came through him could not have been filtered through his consciousness. It was true channeling of the highest quality. We later learned that a dear personal friend of Mr. Greenlee's was framed and went to the penitentiary in the fraud and financial flap that surrounded the I AM group of the Ballards in Chicago some time earlier. Therefore a high quality and clear channel was the only teacher of choice desired by Mr. Greenlee. He had lost a lot of money to the sheer greed of someone in the Chicago group and wasn't ready to allow that to happen again.

Rev. Price was born in Chicago, Illinois, in March of 1889 to circus performer parents. At an early age, he was telling people what was going to happen to them with startling accuracy, much to the deep chagrin of his devout Catholic parents.

When he was seven, they sent him to a Jesuit boarding school with instructions to the fathers there to please exorcise him of these weird and blasphemous talents.

However, the spiritual material that came through him was so interesting and fine, that it caught the attention of two priests, who then, contrarily, took him under their wing and protected him and his talents. As he later declared, "They really were responsible for the better development of my channeling abilities."

He went on through Jesuit schools through the priesthood up to the time of graduation (it is said, to the day of graduation), when he did not appear for his diploma and never did pick it up. Later, he did complete his ministerial studies at the Moody Bible Institute in Chicago and became an ordained minister. He joined the Salvation Army for a short time, but a short-lived marriage did little to keep him there.

While he dearly loved the ministry, teaching, counseling and channeling to help people, his accuracy invariably attracted a substantial group who were most interested in questions of this sort: "Who will win in the fifth at Santa Anita?" and, "Is my sweetheart true to me?"

Since being a minister was a poorly paid position, and the concentration of many of his followers was strictly commercial and mundane, not spiritual, he would give it up and go into business. Several times he became quite wealthy, complete with chauffeur and many other creature comforts.

Then his first love, spiritual teaching, looked better than ever, especially since he could now finance the church himself and hopefully attract a more spiritual group around him. Then, again, discouraged and low on funds, he'd go back into the business world.

At other times, in his desire to find the best way to help people in need, he was a male nurse in a leper colony. He also spent a short time with the Spiritualist group at Lillydale. When Detroit was suffering from a rash of fake psychics, he helped the FBI in their investigations to weed out the unscrupulous.

In a most astonishing case of conscious channeling, he helped one of our friends, who, through fire and the resulting financial complications, had a tremendous business loss for himself and his investors. Consciously, Rev. Price first went through a list of six to eight subsequent offers from across the country which had dead-ended and further upset and confused the friend and his sense of business direction. Rev. Price painted each one in incredible and complete details; he ticked them all off without one question to prompt him. Our friend turned to me and accused me of telling Rev. Price of them. I laughed and said I'd heard from his wife only of the first case. His jaw dropped. "You are right. I stopped telling her about every one because she got much more upset than I did with each subsequent fiasco."

Finally, in his sixties, Rev. Price retired from the public in all ways, except for a very few faithful old students, who had become widely scattered over the years. He was living with his student, Gene Lockhart, in South Bend, Indiana, when the Greenlee's discovered him. After a few meetings with the Greenlee's, and being thoroughly impressed with their deep spiritual purity and intent, he announced, "I will hold back nothing from you. I will help you in every way that I can." He came out of full retirement to bless us all with many of these lessons during the last six years of his life. It was a glorious and wonderful time for this group, a number of whom travelled 50 to 150 miles for the regular meetings. Another couple came 300 miles for stays of up to 10 days and one enthusiastic member came from as far away as Anchorage to stay for months on end.

It was always the desire of Rev. Price to pass away at Christmastime. In December of 1959, he visited one of his students, James Mack, and his family in South Bend, Indiana. As he was preparing for bed on the evening of the 22nd, he fell and suffered a fatal concussion.

The channel's baptismal name was George Graham Price. He was a quiet, humble, but engaging mystic, who won the love and respect of those who crossed his path in life. With his conscious counseling and clairvoyance, he aided many people. His greatest contribution to this world laid in the beautiful lessons that came through him in suspended mental animation.

The name "Frater Achad" in this book can best be understood in terms of "anonymous," as is frequently used by unknown authors of a poem or painting. The term "frater" relates to (fraternal) brother. "Achad" means "one" of the brothers or members of the ancient mystical White Brotherhood, also of the Great High Council members. Therefore the term "Frater Achad" describes one of brothers as the channel.

As a member, he also gave to other members the privilege of the using of his voice box, so that many of the parables and paradoxes in our beloved Bible were made crystal clear in the interpretations given.

The name "Achad" is granted only to those who have given unselfish services to humankind at some time in this life. It is to be used with the greatest discrimination and highest wisdom guidance in their search to serve the Great Council in pure unselfish wisdom.

THE DEDICATED LIFE

O man of Earth! canst thou say
"I am ready, God;
I dedicated my life to Thee?
Use my life as Thou wouldst see,
A benefit that it shall be
To my fellowman.
May my eyes see for Thee
The pain expressed in the urchin's face,
Distress upon the wayward's brow.
Use my feet, O Father God,
That I may walk in paths on Earth
As Thou wouldst have me walk,
That I may carry
Thy message of Light, Thy message of Life,
To man who in darkness dwells.
Use my hands, O Father God,
To reach to them who need Thy help,
To bestow Thy blessings and to receive
Only that, O Lord of Hosts! only that
Which comes from Thee.
Take my life and let it be
Dedicated unto Thee."

CHAPTER ONE

THE ANCIENT MYSTICAL WHITE BROTHERHOOD, AFTER THE ORDER OF MELCHIZEDEK

There is but one race — the human race
There is but one man — Godman
There is but one life — Godlife
There is but one mind — Godmind.

Ever since man has been, the ancient mystical White Brotherhood after the Order of Melchizedek has been. It is spiritual as God is spiritual. It is birthless, ageless, and deathless as God is birthless, ageless, and deathless. It is not a mundane organization, having no earthly lodges nor any material buildings or churches made of brick, steel, or stone. It is not founded on any man-made dogma, creed, or ritual. It is free from any

1

influence or persuasion, and its authority and power come from the eternal Divine Source of pure being.

The word "Melchizedek" is the only one all-inclusive word for the brotherhood of man. In Hebrew, it is a combination of two words: "Melchi," meaning king, and "Zedek," meaning righteousness, the right use of consciousness and all our mental faculties. (Heb. 7:1-3)

Members of the ancient mystical White Brotherhood, after the Order of Melchizedek, are myriad in number and are invisible to the human eye. They are very high spiritual beings from many planets of the universe, including this planet Earth. These highly evolved great ones are of superior character, extremely wise, and express divine intelligence beyond our mortal comprehension. They always work together as one. There are many ways they use to convey their instruction when it is necessary to use the vibration of sound. They are able to speak the language of any race or nation that they are contacting and with whom they are working. They work mainly from the exalted supernatural planes of divine intelligence.

They are aware at all times what is transpiring on our Earth and are in constant communication, on the inner planes of life, with other members of the Order, and of those of the subordinate planes of the Brotherhood. Nothing is hidden from them; they are always aware of what is taking place and read the motives of mankind behind the actions even before they have taken place.

Members of the White Brotherhood who have risen to the Melchizedek plane are referred to as sons of God. In very ancient times, the first governors of nations and races were Melchizedek priests and kings. (They are referred to as having Divine authority.) They were sent by the high principle of life, the "I AM," to perform these duties to establish moral law and order for the protection and benefit of humanity.

These members were always noble, spiritual entities and were regarded as possessing the divine authority to so rule. Their decisions were never questioned, because their decisions and judgments were always just.

There are many degrees, planes, or levels in the White Brotherhood. In the category of learning for souls seeking illumination, there are also many levels, as in our schools of the mundane or earthly schools. We have the lower grades and the higher grades of education, such as high school, colleges, and universities. Likewise, the ancient White Brotherhood have these various levels of advancement on the inner planes of consciousness. As the consciousness is expanded, its growth covers unlimited fields of operation that are vast in scope and dimension.

Teachers on one plane of consciousness receive their instructions from those of a higher plane of greater light and divine wisdom. This limitless spiral of ascension goes on and on, ever upward, outward into the vastness of eternal light, for there is no end to

3

truth and light. Never will there be an end, for the end is ever the beginning.

Within the White Brotherhood, the plane referred to as "after the Order of Melchizedek" is the highest plane that humanity is able mortally to understand. On this plane, members know, understand, and use all the immutable laws of life, love, and creation, righteously so. Its members are assigned to teach and enlighten the leaders of Earth, seers, prophets, kings, presidents, educators, philosophers, etc. They always guide through inspiration, and teach and counsel those leaders in key positions with the purest of spiritual intelligence and divine wisdom, always pointing to the great eternal purposes of humanity's cyclic movements. The assistance they give helps those who seek their aid and accomplishes the greatest spiritual advancement for humankind.

Within the White Brotherhood, there is a council which is composed of master teachers of all eras of time. Within this body of exalted, illumined beings, many decisions are formulated. As the Council looks beyond the present into that which man of Earth calls the future, the decisions made serve the greatest good for the greatest need of mankind — soul growth. Quite frequently, when progress seems the most retarded to human reasoning, the Council (seeing the horizon far beyond that which is known or visible to mortal sight) knows that this is the time when the greatest spiritual action is taking place within the affairs of men.

This is why the Council is very careful in making selections of men or women for key positions of trust. Only those are selected who have discharged all their karmic indebtedness to anyone or any race. Thus they are not in bondage to any man of Earth and are beyond the corruption of mortal thinking or mortal influence and persuasion. Those who qualify are always just, honorable, stand on principle, and have no fear of anything. They are properly trained and equipped with talents necessary for their duties. This training might not be visible on the surface, for it was accomplished on the inner planes of life. They are ready for the service to be rendered. They are those with whom the Council can work from the unseen side of life, through inspiration, within the realms of spiritual consciousness. They are those who are placed in vital key positions.

Wherever the voice of one of the great ones is heard, through any avenue, the values of life take on a new meaning and direction. Thus man of Earth is able to see and understand the outcome of certain actions taken, whenever the divine guidance of the Council is followed in preference to that of mortal reasoning. Its ultimate conclusions always contribute to the advancement of man's moral character and spiritual stature, for he has gained greater spiritual insight.

The teachings of these great divine teachers have been known for thousands of years. The most ancient records reveal the presence of these great ones in old

5

Chaldean times, in Egypt, and in Persia. The records reveal that they were always referred to as the "Brotherhood of Mankind." They foretold that many of their order would come, and they spoke of a "master of masters" who would enlighten humanity to a far greater degree than those who proceeded him. He would be a high priest, after the Order of Melchizedek. They prophesied that he, too, would be born of a woman as other great ones before him. He, as they, would be born under spiritual, mystical circumstances. His birth, life, and purpose would be announced by the angelic heavenly hosts.

All members of this high ancient mystical White Brotherhood are no longer inhabitants of a physical habiliment. The vehicles these divine teachers used were of no earthly forms, but were of etheric bodies; therefore they were always referred to in our sacred books and holy writs as angels or heavenly hosts. They always radiated such tremendous lines of force and power, even though they were invisible to the human eye, that their influence and presence was felt unmistakably. Only those of inherent sensitivity were able to discern their presence. Those of lesser perception or sensitivity were unable to see or feel them.

All master teachers and great initiates are in this Melchizedek Council. It is an eternal priesthood, but it is not after any man-made organization. This eternal priesthood is "after the Order of Melchizedek," which is birthless, ageless, and deathless. (Heb. 6 and 7.)

Any soul that was part of this Earth plane and its experiences, and which reached this highest plane of consciousness called the "Melchizedek Order," has reached it through a dedicated life of unselfish service to God, during many incarnations. Asking no praise, power, or recognition, but having the inner awareness of the all-pervading, immutable principles of pure being, the Christ-consciousness, the Godmind is self-realized and established.

That soul, while on Earth, ruled his or her life from the place of the "Most High" in righteousness. The conscious and subconscious activities were geared to peace, love, and wisdom. That soul let the superconscious mind or divine mind flow unobstructed in completeness. In other words, there was a complete surrender to God's will, the will of good only. This is the order that Jesus belonged to and ruled in as Christ Jesus, the high priest forever, after the Order of Melchizedek. (Heb. 10:16.)

The Melchizedek Council is a most high truth-revealing tribunal, their services and teachings are always as "unto the one eternal God." Knowing that God's will is the only perfect will, any assignment that is given to a member or a teacher on a slightly lower plane of the great White Brotherhood always has a definite spiritual purpose. The reasons for this are to aid the various races of humanity raise their consciousness level, and to develop their perceptions of their own divine, inherent nature.

7

All master teachers of the Melchizedek Order have pointed to the fact that man is a triune being, following the triune principle of life: first, man is spirit, one with life, since there is no separation in God; second, man is a soul, in which God-mind is individualized; third, man has a house of clay, a vehicle in which he operates, a body composed of matter which he uses to serve God and which he needs to prove the principles of life as a Godman.

There are many fine spiritual teachers who are working on the lower levels of the White Brotherhood, who are serving the great ones, to inspire others, to point the way of service toward the higher regions of work. Members of the Brotherhood who were on the Earth plane and who now serve on the upper levels of authority, know the immutable Laws of the Universe. They, too, have passed every test in life, having paid all indebtedness of karma of their previous unregenerated lives. They steadfastly and sincerely kept their standards high, never compromising on any principles of life and truth. Their lives were dedicated to pure, unselfish service and beheld all life as God-life. It is thus they kept the "whiteness of their soul" and qualified to be admitted to the higher levels, or Order of the ancient mystical White Brotherhood. No one can ever be a member of the White Brotherhood who deliberately uses any of the immutable laws for prestige or power, for personal gain or advancement, who exploits any man of Earth unfairly and unjustly, who uses deception in any form to misrepresent or confuse. If it is not of God, it is not spiritual, therefore it is not of the White Brotherhood.

All master teachers of old, including those we are more familiar with, such as Abraham, Amenhotep of Egypt, Gautama Buddha, Confucius, Krishna, Enoch, Daniel, Jesus, Zoroaster, Pythagoras, Plato, Aristotle, and many other myriad teachers of old, as well as many of more recent times, were members of the White Brotherhood and shall continue to be so forever.

Who tenanted a body first? What was it that tenanted a body of these wonderful teachers? It was the I AM which is the Christ-light or Christ-power of God. It has always been and shall always be the I AM or the Christ-light of God, which spoke in every teacher who carried the torch of truth, even though it was unrecognized by those who heard them. It shall continue to ever be that I AM, the Christ-light of God, speaking in all teachers of the living God, yesterday, today, and in the future.

Just as Abraham was the Christ-light of God to his people, and the teacher Confucius was the Christ-light of God to his people, Zoroaster was the Christ-light of God to his people, even as Gautama Buddha of India and Jesus of Nazareth were each the Christ-light of God to their people in their time.

The presiding elders of the White Brotherhood are the Master Jesus and the beloved Gautama Buddha. They are the presiding elders because they are the

9

supreme teachers in the service of the great Cosmic Father.

There is but one man, Godman. Let no man of Earth, in his limited understanding, tell you otherwise, for he or she who so attempts to do is speaking in error, contrary to truth. All are in the One and the One is eternally in all, all One.

All great spiritual teachers recognize this true eternal principle of the brotherhood of man, the completeness of creation in the vastness of life. Life is complete. However, man must first become aware of this completeness, and this he will do when he ascends in consciousness enough to comprehend the vastness of his own divinity. Very few of those who heard the messages fully understood the meaning, nor were they able to grasp the meaning of the unity of the human race in the spiritual realms.

These great initiates and sages are still continuing to teach in the bright light of the oversoul of the universe, known to man of Earth as God. You will understand there is nothing impossible for the master teachers or the Council members to accomplish. They are those who have finished their travail upon the mundane sphere of life, having learned well how the immutable laws operate, therefore, having no further desires, there is no necessity to return in physical habiliment or earthly form. This is because they are now in a field of activity where they are of far greater service in the Father's realm and can reach more people through the vibratory power of love and the constructive energy forces of their good will in spiritual guidance.

There are many subordinate teachers on the lower planes or regions of the great White Brotherhood. These teachers are not to be confused with those of Melchizedek realm. These subordinate teachers are not immediately affiliated with the inner Council of the Melchizedek realm, but receive their instructions from the outer Council. They are not to be held in lesser regard. This is to be understood and respected very clearly. They are to be regarded in their full spiritual importance, as they receive their instructions for their assigned duties from those of the outer Council, who have in turn received their information from the inner Council. These subordinate teachers are entirely devoted to reaching others in love and are to be looked upon as those in the earthly schools, teachers teaching "babes" in their various degrees of unfoldment in the matter of the inner life of the soul. All mankind must be reached in love, all are loved of God and are equals in spiritual inheritance. All must be awakened to the immutable laws that govern them. There lies the work for the laborers of the field, so that all may claim their eternal inheritance, when they have merited it through acceptance and cooperation.

We quite often hear the statement made by misinformed individuals on the mundane sphere of life, that, "It is impossible for the higher teachers to pene-

11

trate the denser forms of matter." There is no matter too dense for any great teacher to penetrate! The only dense form of matter which the master's lesson or instructions do not penetrate is man's thinking. This is stated in love and not in any measure of destructive criticism. It is only when man rejects the light of truth, for there is no greater blindness than the blindness of one who will not see.

Why does the White Brotherhood have so many subordinate teachers? All must grow, and it is for that reason some of the instructions are passed onto the more recently arrived souls from the Earth plane, who have expressed a desire to become teachers, to guide others of the Earth plane, loved ones they have left behind, to help them understand the true light of God. Thus they too may enjoy the opportunity of soul growth and, in this manner, prepare themselves, while they are in the astral embodiment, waiting for their return to the Earth and mundane life, where they will again tenant a physical body.

Many of these teachers, through their soul's desire for greater illumination, longed to have the experience of direct contact with the spiritual realms, the inner life. They were collaborators with the White Brotherhood. This can only come about when they have given recognition to the vast spiritual teachings of the Council members of ancient age. Through the recognition of the eternal truths and light of these teachings, these subordinate teachers progressed in their wisdom and

12

evolvement and eventually attained mastership in their own right.

When the members of the ancient mystical White Brotherhood dwelt among men of Earth in a physical body, it was their desire to teach man of Earth of his true relationship to and with God, which is spiritual. When a member found, at the time of his leaving the body, after his transition, that his work was still unaccomplished, he or she continued on the inner planes of life until they had some avenue to accomplish this unfinished business. They would work from the unseen side of life through the process of inspiration directed to a dedicated, open-minded soul free of selfish motives; a willing physical collaborator who could reach and influence those who needed help.

It has been erroneously said that this opening of oneself to be used as a channel, could lead to obsession by some astral, earthbound soul. He who is dedicated to God, spiritual and pure in consciousness, with unselfish motives in his thinking, has nothing to fear of any obsession. The Brotherhood will not stand idly by and see this happen. There is nothing to fear of the discarnate soul. It is the soul still incarnate in the flesh that needs to be guarded against. Like attracts like, the magnet of love attracts love; the forces of hatred and contempt attract destruction in a human being, by focusing his attention to it consciously or unconsciously. According to their desire and their free will, it will be done.

13

These great masters and sages of old recognize man's every good deed, kindly act, and loving word here in the material world. This is particularly true of those who have accepted the beneficence of the illumined, the appointed and annointed masters, and their teachings of the principles of life. The time has come for seekers of the truth of being to step out of the swaddling clothes of old, worn-out concepts and theologies, full of fear and superstitions which have held them in bondage of fear of the eternal. Man must know that he is free in the fullness of God and is given free will to choose the path in which he wishes to gather the results of accumulated experiences needed to gain wisdom. He must also ever be mindful that, in this freedom, he is always fully responsible for his choice, to himself, his fellow man, as well as to the Creator, and that no one has the right to deny or destroy another's right to that same freedom. Injustice, in any capacity, is no man's right.

One of the first steps in soul growth is the disciplining of the emotional nature of man. Disciplining means learning by the application of truths learned through meditation, prayers, doing, living, controlling your actions and reaction. These lead to the purification of not only the physical centers of the body, but the etheric centers. Man is full of many complexes, attitudes and desires based on intellectual reasoning. By continuing his dedication, he is led until the purification of the centers is accomplished and they are as

14

lighted candles on the altar of God. Many of these souls are quite frequently unnoticed among men of Earth; they could be friends, co-workers, neighbors, or loved ones close by who are being prepared for some greater service in the Father's house.

We have heard the term, "crashing or storming the gates of heaven." There is no climbing over the wall or crashing of the gate, for the gate opens only to him who has gone through the purification and dedication of his life, having walked the path of service and love. Intellectual knowledge, wishes, and desires alone will not do it. The spiral of love and service is an ascending spiral ever penetrating level after level with both the inner and outer awareness of the all-pervading essence of pure being. In modern understanding, the passing through the gate is a breakthrough in consciousness, the initiation to higher levels of intelligence and spiritual perception.

There is only one ascension and that is the ascension in consciousness. When the soul comprehends the true purposes of life, the controlling principles, the divine plan of unfoldment, it is illumined, or "Christed;" the Godmind has taken full control and as Paul said, "Let that mind be in you which was in Christ Jesus." Thus man becomes a member of the great White Brotherhood with an opportunity for higher growth under the Melchizedek Order. He is now aware of his union with God, his true selfhood in the white light of God, a radiant son, and as a son of

15

God he is immersed, submerged in the pure presence of the great oversoul of life, which we call God.

Man never ceases to serve. He shall use the creative laws of the universe to still troubled water, to enlighten confused thinking, heal the discomfort of broken bodies, remove obstacles to spiritual growth; he shall use these laws lovingly and constructively always. Never, never does he use them to retard anyone for selfish reasons or gain, never for power, position, or reward, and at all times gives man the opportunity to redeem himself for his erroneous actions.

There are isolated instances when it becomes necessary for members of the Council, the great initiates, to return to the Earth plane of life and assume a body of flesh to complete special divine assignments left undone by others, quite frequently that of a collaborator of the Brotherhood. They do this when it is a vital matter.

For eons of time, many master teachers have been known to make unprecedented appearances. Often they arrive in unexpected places unannounced and depart in the same manner. The body which a member uses frequently bears the resemblance of the last personality which the member used while on the Earth plane. The body is not always of the dense physical form, but rather an etheric body, having the semblance of an earthly body. The body may appear at will and can be shed at will. It can seemingly disappear from human sight only to make a reappearance when it is needed. Each appears to a collaborator or a teacher with whom he can work, giving him the spiritual insight, aid, and assistance in some very outstanding endeavor for the benefit of humankind. Members of the White Brotherhood never announce their true identity to any one; they never speak of their particular service which they render, nor do they reveal what their mission is. Silence and humility is ever their watchword and their silent influence is felt by all whom they contact personally, as well as those fortunate enough to come into the radiance of their spiritual auric vehicle.

The members of this White Brotherhood embrace all mankind regardless of race, color, or creed. However, they do not accept anyone as a teacher or a collaborator who is allied with those who conform to that which is contrary to truth, contrary to God's law. This is found in some earthly organizations who claim an affiliation, yet their precepts and very actions are contrary to God's laws of being.

Many of the members of the White Brotherhood walked the Earth sphere of life as we do now. They, too, have tasted of the bitter cup, as the great Gautama Buddha, the Illumined One, also as Confucius, the Appointed One, and our beloved Jesus of Nazareth, the Anointed One. Many of the collaborators who are now about the Father's business also have tasted of the sweet and the bitter cup; therefore life is no longer a mystery to them. They have learned to be tolerant, patient, and now understand the reason for many things and experiences. (Eccl. 7:25.)

God asks for no sacrifice; mercy is the plea of God and the Council, mercy was the plea of all great teachers of their time, and they still continue to teach mercy and love. As the Nazarene said, "I ask not for sacrifice, I ask but for mercy." God is love, and, "He who loveth is born of God." To be born (the second birth) is to be sustained, carried by grace, fed by inspiration, led by guidance and inspired by divine spirit.

While man lives in his physical body, he is often given over to strange notions. (That is the so-called denser side of matter.) Man never becomes perfectly free from the astral shell, which he builds for himself out of every thought, word, and deed while he occupies his time in the physical world. This astral shell conveys him after his transition. Man, in his rebellion, clings to many of these peculiar and strange notions, contrary to truth. Therefore it necessitates incarnations, birth after birth (name it as you will) until at last man becomes free from all material superstitions and on the road where he will discard all mental obstructions. Then he will be weaving together the threads he gathered in the shuttle across the loom of life, for he will be finishing the pattern of his life's record.

The ancient mystical White Brotherhood teaches that man of Earth should not aspire to rank, station, prestige, or power. All mankind should seek the one great asset, which is humility. Unselfishness and love shall reign supreme without discrimination.

When men of Earth shall see other men of Earth as spiritual beings, there need never be any fear of the future. Even though man may be in tatters and rags, or perchance clothed in garments of wealth; yellow, black, or brown of skin; it is not the outer appearance in which man shall be interested. It is the inner spiritual being, the Christ power working through that physical body which should occupy and hold his attention.

There are many men and women walking along the highway of life in shabby or ragged attire. They have faces and hands soiled from toil, but their hearts are clean and pure. Conversely, there are those whose bodies are in silks and satins and know not that they are in truth equal with the beggars; because their hearts are not clean and pure. Remember and never forget, they are all spiritual beings, children of the Living God. Therefore let there be no discrimination.

Ever remember that members of the White Brotherhood are always creators of good will, harmony, and love, never strife nor deception, being advocates of the living, radiant light of divine love. They always encourage the noblest attributes in others, and they frequently strive to inspire man toward perfecting the spiritual growth by applying the understanding he has

19

and appropriating its resulting wisdom in his consciousness.

Quite frequently, the question is raised as to the reference of the word "White". That reference has nothing to do with the color of the skin or to any race. It does indicate the radiance of the spiritual color of the soul (its aura). It indicates the pureness of the love expressed by the soul's divinity. The Divine wears many colored bodies. It is the heart which must be "white" or pure and not what we hear referred to as "black-hearted," or corrupt, no matter what the color of the skin may be, white, or some other color.

God is no respecter of persons and in God there is no separation. Since God is both male and female in principle, and principle is sexless, God expresses the divine nature of both male and female. The Council is also a part of God, and it also makes no discrimination. There are female masters just as there are male. The male members are referred to as fraters and the female members are sorers. In the etheric planes of life, all members are recognized as fraters, meaning brothers; for in the realm of pure consciousness of spirit, the recognition is of the spirit which is sexless, thus the recognition is as equals in all attributes (Matt. 22:30.)

There is a sacred duty the sorors render to motherhood on Earth; it is what is frequently referred to as the Nature's Mothering principle of life, that principle which sustains, nourishes, and lovingly protects. The sorors lovingly grant this service. One of the greatest tasks is in the watching over the young mothers during the gestation and the final coming forth of the body of the babe. Also, another one of the tasks among the women collaborators is to minister unto the children and youth in the many organizations, institutions, and hospitals of the physical plane of life. They are always there to give aid and assistance.

The master Jesus said, "I go to prepare a place for you, that where I am, there you may also be." They have a place prepared. Each one whom they call and who has chosen to follow the call is precious to the Council. There is a path of direction for each one. If it were not so, there would be no calling of man to come up higher to serve in the Father's mansion, the universe.

Man cannot serve until there is a necessity for service. As the necessity arises, each one that they have called stands ready to answer the summons. spread the love of God wherever you can. Whatever you do, do it lovingly. Love is the greatest power in the universe. thus many experiences of life appear as what man calls miracles. Love sent forth brought about the seeming miracles.

Love becomes a great magnetic power and draws unto itself still greater essence of the presence of God. As the masters of old lived their portion of life serving others as "unto God," so continue to help others to

behold all life as God's life, and they, too, shall serve
as "unto God."

Natasha Greenlee

CHAPTER TWO

CALLING COLLABORATORS AND TEACHERS

One of the Brotherhood speaks:

Why do we, of the Council of the ancient mystical White Brotherhood, wend our way back? We will not have man floundering around in the recesses of darkness when there is an opportunity for us to shed light. Eventually, man must have no darkness in which to hide or scamper into, and we are referring to the darkness of ignorance and superstition. For back and back and back over the treadmill of life man passes until he becomes weary of darkness, of selfishness and ignorance and calls for enlightenment.

23

We, of the Council of the ancient mystical White Brotherhood, over eons of time, seek and search and find acceptable teachers, and this does not happen in just a day, week, month or year. All mankind is destined to serve God. Those who are to serve God in the full measure of Divine Stewardship, are those who have traveled across life's sands many, many times. It is for that reason many have been called, but very few choose to answer that call immediately. All ultimately will and do answer, but it takes time.

It is always our desire to keep each individual, to a greater degree, upon their own independence. It would not be a difficult matter for those of our Council to reveal in detail to you how conditions and circumstances here on the mundane sphere of life would eventually come to a climax. It is our desire, moreover, that those whom we choose travel the path without seeing the complete picture, as it were. This results in an incentive for those called to move forward in faith, that soul will get its full reward spiritually.

However, when one who has been called, who has chosen to follow the path of love and light, finds the path becoming a trifle darkened and we can be of assistance, we do shed some ray of light, as it is our duty so to do. We are interested, divinely interested, and for that reason we shall see no shadows cross the path of those called. We shall see no obstacles remain in the path, for he or she who zealously serves God is worthy of every respect and consideration.

We are interested in teachers, teachers, and more teachers, and we cannot find them fast enough. The wheat fields are ready to be reaped and thrashed, and the vines are laden with grapes ready to be garnered. We are in need of workers and there are still many who are running the gamut, as it were, of the treadmill of worn-out, threadbare orthodoxy.

Step by step, we shall lead you. The victor becomes a victor only when he invades the enemy's camp, particularly the enemy's camp within his own thought process. We shall lead you. We read an unfinished scroll, and we know there is much work to be done. In this very hour, there are many who are treading along life's path seeking, knocking, asking. What are they seeking? Light! Whom and where are they seeking from? God! Upon whose door are they knocking? Upon the door of the inner chamber of their storehouse where there is a plenteous supply of God's substance.

Are they to continue to seek, continue to knock? For what are they asking? Release from strife, release from the bondage of mortal chaos.

Each one of you has carried a cross, and upon that cross has hung your spiritual body, and in that spiritual body you have kneeled and have called to us, your elder brothers, for assistance, which is always granted.

Perchance there be those who have made a choice to follow the path of light and love, in service to humankind, and later found through impatience that the road is too long and that the rocks, which they have placed in the road themselves, scarred their feet, and they no longer desire to travel that road, but seek another. We, of the Council, never bind; we bind no man of earth.

Man is only happy when he enjoys the freedom in that which he is doing, just as you enjoy your freedom in that which you are doing now. Should there be any remaining rocks in your path, rocks or obstructions of the past, they shall become as dust beneath your feet, and you shall brush them aside quite lightly. Should there be thorns or nettles of the past, which have tired your souls, they too shall be dissolved and no longer shall you feel the hurt of their pricks. They shall become as ointment, or as oil of love, for you shall know you are accomplishing another overcoming. Bind not, dear hearts of Earth; let man live freely, let man give freely.

As in your soul's consciousness, those of you who have accepted the call, so you serve. Should there be those who, on hearing the call and making the choice to serve, as "unto God," and then because of some desire or reason of their own, they turn to another road, they shall never, never travel beyond our watchful eye. We do not forsake, we have no locks upon the door of the chamber of the Council of the ancient mystical White Brotherhood. It is never closed, it stands open and he who chooses to enter, may choose to leave.

Do not bind another, and in love, you cannot bind; man, Godman, is free.

We desire that you understand fully the immensity of the task which lies before each collaborator. However, it shall not be a task, it shall be a duty performed in love, and the beauty of love shall come forth as you continue in your paths of service.

Each one we have chosen to serve with us shall serve, after he has made his choice within his inner consciousness to follow the light. Quite often, it takes a little time, as you call it, for man of Earth to make up his mind, as to what he desires to do. When we make a choice, we look beyond the present into that which man of Earth calls the future. When progress seems the most retarded, that is the time when the greatest spiritual action is taking place within.

We never become involved with mortal confusion; we know nothing of it. We are aware that man lives in a physical habiliment and is subject, to a degree, to the environment of the mortal or physical plane. We do our best to enlighten him as to how he shall rise from that portion of life's pattern he has made of his own choosing. We never attempt to help without knowing that there is an end to man's mortal chaos.

All the instructions on the immutable laws or principles that we have endeavored to share with some of our collaborators were given so that they might be broadcast to others and reach those who need its lesson and information to solve their mortal chaos. Distress of the physical body is an evidence of accumulated error, but does not, by necessity, have to remain. It can be overcome.

Man of Earth has made this statement, "Thoughts are things." We say, "Thoughts become things." Thus man endures for a brief season after he has placed his foot in the right direction upon the road of God's truth and abides by the immutable laws that govern that truth.

We have made this statement, "Let there be a smile in man's voice." First, however, man must learn to smile in his thinking. For man's thinking is evidence in speech, words, deeds, and acts. The Galilean understood this when he said, "Man liveth not by bread alone, but by every word which proceedeth forth from the mouth of God."

Dear hearts, there is no separation in God, for remember you are within that realm of God. We, too, are a part of God. Therefore do not look upon one with greater favor than the other. Remember, since God is no respecter of persons, neither are we of the Council.

When you survey the scene you will find, as the Nazarene, so do we make our choice from what man calls "all walks of life." It necessitates experience; man must have experience. Memory never dies. However, remember this and never forget it: never disturb the waters when they are placid and cheerful to the eye by looking back into the memories of the past, recalling old doubts, fears, unhappy experiences, permitting them to enter your thinking. Never, never look back, not even for a tiny peek, for it is as having cleansed the room of your home thoroughly, then bringing back the dirt and rubbish into the room and corrupting its orderliness. Never draw back old karma into your memory, lest you make new karma in doing so and need to undo that again. There is no greater peace for man's soul than having lived honestly, having remained true to his noble, immortal self.

We make this statement in love, the love of the living God. We have been interested in leading man for eons of time. We have many collaborators through which we reach others and attract them to walk the path of light. We are preparing to permeate the mundane sphere of life with well-rounded truths. Theology is serving its purpose. It has proven to be a stepping-stone for man while traversing the physical plane of life. We have been making these preparations over eons of time, and now it becomes necessary for the ushering in of the new concept for the enlightenment of mankind. Remember our work is spiritual and not to be considered as merely religious. All mankind can apply these principles regardless of his choice of devotion to his God.

That which is done in accord with divine law can never go amiss. That which is done contrary to divine law, regardless of what walk of life it may be, suffers its own consequences.

The morsels of truth, which the teachers have shared unselfishly with others, have proven to be as a beacon light on a rugged coast along the way. All such effort has not been in vain, for as truth is shared with others, the listener, in turn, shares it and thus the endless chain of love is formed.

There are no plans to be made for immediate procedure, for remember, plans are not necessary when desire is righteous. Plans quite often savor of misguidance of the unregenerated centers. You have acquired knowledge, and the knowledge which you have acquired has led you into the path of wisdom. Now the Godman, of which you are a part, is beginning to enfold you in the fullness of that divine principle.

We never find fault with anyone, and we make every allowance for mortal restlessness. In choosing our physical collaborators, we know that, in due time, mortal restlessness will be overcome. Because of the frailty of what you have learned to call human nature, men of earth will, at times, be prone to doubt the veracity of some of our statements and predictions; therefore we make this statement lovingly: remember, faith is the substance of things (desired or) hoped for, the evidence of things not seen. Faith will attract from the vastness of the Cosmos, the manifestation into reality in the physical form. Let that be your watchword, faith.

When we, of the Council, make statements that seem to mortal reasoning utterly impossible, have faith, for God's law is a natural law. Experience, as you already know, is a great teacher. It is born of wisdom, and wisdom means success and knows no defeat. As each soul applies the lessons he has learned through experience, tolerance is born. Where tolerance is, there can never be negligence. Restlessness is a mortal attribute and restlessness shall soon be forgotten when hands and feet become busy.

Remember, it is not who man is. It is what man is! The "who" is the mortal personality; and the "what" is the spiritual individuality which is Godman. We, of the Council, always endeavor to quicken the Godman in each soul's consciousness, through the encouragement of the "what" man is, and not the "who" man is. We do not give recognition to the mortal personality; we are not interested in mortal personalities. They do not interest us. Mortal personalities are ephemeral and are but figments of mental emotions, mental frustrations, mortally so only. We are trying to make this very plain to you, to enlighten you, to lead you to the "what" you are. Those who are coming into the fullness of this light are becoming attracted. Those who are expressing their desire to be mundane collaborators, workers in the Father's vineyards, they are Israelitish; meaning, willing to travel the path of spiritual light.

Now, let us again make a distinction between personality and individuality. Personalities change; individuality never changes. It cannot change because it is the indwelling, incarnate principle of God. That ever-present, ever-prevailing power of God is individualized in you as God in action.

Do not be unmindful of the Law of Attraction. Throughout the length and breadth of this universe, there are both men and women waiting to share their ideas and their efforts, where their ideas may become fruitful for the cause of dedicated unselfish services to mankind.

No man is barred as a collaborator because of his religious belief. As man is called to become a collaborator and makes his choice to follow, he makes the adjustments between truth and error within his own inner being of consciousness. If he is unwilling to accept the truth of God as the truth of God is taught through enlightened teachers, he must remain the "who" of personality only, for he or she has not found the eternal "what" that he is. We pronounce no judgment and we inflict no condemnation ever, nor do we expect to find any condemnation arising from among our chosen collaborators. The calling of collaborators here on your earth plane is the only means of expression we have to voice the message of the immortality of life, which is God in action, in abundance.

We make this next statement in love. If we, of the Council, were to keep record or give countenance to the paths through which our collaborators have passed, we would be without physical collaborators.

The "what," or the spirit of man answers and makes the choice of what he shall do and how he shall serve, always in obedience to the eternal laws of God, for he is ordained by God. That is the only ordination that we recognize. Whenever man is interested in lifting another man from sorrow or strife, regardless of the name of the organization with which he is allied, he is recognized by we, of the Council of the ancient mystical White Brotherhood. "Seek and you shall find; knock and the door shall be opened; ask and it shall be given unto you." Remember, there are no closed doors to God.

God's law is a gracious law; God's law is not mandatory. It is free and does not restrict or bind. Man has free will. Now, when we find one of the Earth who should be about his Father's business, and we find him at that particular progress along life's path where his debts become due and payable, it is then we call that one, and he is granted every opportunity to pay all the debts of past mistakes.

Here is where the greatest tests are. Choices are made, and if man endures his experiences of paying of debts, in tolerance, with wisdom, he passes spiritually through the gate, not over the wall, and he is then recognized as a bearer of light, a messenger of light and truth; for he is setting an example for others, through his integrity, his character and his path of unselfish service. (St. John 10:1)

Only those are attracted to such services who are ready and have been given proper instructions. We have those in our Council who are very capable of inspiring the mundane collaborators. That is why we are very careful in making our selection for key positions of trust. Though there may be a few spots on the inside of the vessel of a man (personality with its peculiar notions), we have the greatest scouring powder of the universe to scour and remove all blemishes, or spots of character.

We shall not select too many vessels, or pots with grave blemishes in them, let us assure you. Injustice is no man's right, and he or she who claims injustice digs his own pitfall.

We shall never permit betrayal, mark you this well. Remember the words of the ancient sage when he said, "He kept the whiteness of his soul and over him, men wept." Therefore, keep the whiteness of your soul. We seek to ordain shepherds for the flock, who shall feed the sheep and His lambs. The lambs and the yearlings, we ask that you shelter against your breast. Love knows no end. Caesar has no power to defeat. What can defeat God's immutable, infinite Law of Love?

You are familiar with the saying of old, "Coming events cast their shadow before." The hour has been approaching, and it is at hand. There are many who are now among you that are not here on the mundane sphere of life to accomplish material or physical ends.

34

The power of God is not to be disregarded. Man of earth shall not desecrate his spiritual obligation, and it is indeed a spiritual obligation with the creative principle of life.

Those of you who are now radiating love in your aura shall need very little help from us, as far as you individually are concerned, but so far as the contamination of others in the distortion of truth is concerned, we assure you now, there we shall help you.

Life is birthless, ageless, deathless. God is birthless, ageless, deathless. Never, never is there an end; there is no end. There is no end either physically or spiritually. There are changes, transmutations from one form to another, but no annihilation due to the principle of true being. Now listen to us, please: many of you who have been chosen have come from various walks of life, and that needs must be. It is better for men to have experiences traveling the path of their own lives, each in his own way, than for us to have made the choice of those who are traveling in but one direction. As we have mentioned before, experience is the greatest teacher which leads to wisdom and that action which shall spell success and tolerance.

Listen, let us come back to God. God makes no demands! God does not command! Your acceptance of our fellowship with you in the ancient mystical White Brotherhood, would be in this wise; to the principles of truth, you say aye, and to error, you would say nay, and that is not by word of mouth to any one of us invisible elder brothers, as we are frequently referred to. Then where would you say aye and nay? Ah, our beloved of God; within the sanctum sanctorum of your soul's consciousness. Your God is the one and only universal God. Whether your neighbor accepts your God with equal measure with you or the man or woman with whom you brush elbows while walking down the path of life, your God remains your God, unmoved and unchanged.

Your heaven remains your heaven and your God is principle. Heaven is a state of consciousness and since principle cannot be changed, your God cannot be changed.

Remember, there are no enemies. You have no enemies, only as in your thinking you give recognition to enmity. You cannot be held accountable for the manner in which your fellowman thinks. That is not your responsibility. If a man thinks in terms of enmity toward you and so expresses himself and you accept it, then you become a part of the bargain of enmity, do you not? There shall never be any need for you to become emotionally disturbed, only as you desire to be. We realize that it is rather difficult for man of Earth to endure patience. Remember, never forget, be unmindful of public opinion, but be ever mindful of the truth of the principle of God, which never changes. Have courage; have all courage; it is a priceless treasure and never loses its power, for it is of God.

As a tiny seed dropped in fertile soil, so will your acts of love help and lead your fellowman "From the unreal to the real, from darkness into light; from death unto immortality and life." Your acts of love will have nurtured the seeds and they will bear fruitage.

It is always necessary to have material or physical sustenance to carry out a well-formed desire. That is not contrary to the law of abundance; it is within the realm of right and justice that it should be so. It is also well that man conform himself to the established laws of the country in which he lives. This we do not only advocate, but this we recognize as the pinnacle of truth. However, it is unfortunate that that which man has learned to call physical government has fallen into the care and keeping of many unscrupulous individuals.

Why do people become unscrupulous? Mainly for the reason that they are young in soul growth. There are always those who shall cross their path, who desire to shed the light of truth, but because of the infancy in soul growth, they reject the truth. This does not become the crime, as it were, or the responsibility of the teacher. It remains the debt of the rejector.

Remember, as spiritual teachers, you shall, in obedience, conform to man-made laws. As we have stated before, it is unfortunate that God's laws must be in submission to mortal laws, that the laws of God may be taught; the laws of truth and righteousness, the principles of God are a law unto themselves. Hold fast to these principles and your ship shall never encounter the rocks of despair. It is blessed that you keep nestled within the bosom of each one of you the oil of love. Nurture it. For you are placing the toe of the foot of your understanding into the pool of the vastness of the eternal cosmos. Keep the oil of understanding clean and pure, so that when the pillars of the new temple of your soul are placed, they shall not decay or crumble.

Now, let it be understood, we do not demand ministers. For have we not mentioned that there are many more ministers who walk the highways and the byways of life, than stand in the pulpit or edifices made of stone, wood, steel and brick? Whenever a man is interested in lifting another from sorrow or strive, his love of service makes him a minister of God — yes!

In the abiding ever-present presence of the living Christ of God, we know you who chose to serve, for as you have crossed life's span, you have not walked alone. The great purpose of the return of the teachers of our side of life to the mundane spheres is to enlighten man and not to keep him in darkness for eons of time. Were man properly taught, life would long ago have been easier and sweeter. Chaos and strife can never remain permanent. Man will learn that his greatest enemy is his own thinking.

We, of the Council, who are able to come back to visit and work with man of Earth, we, too, had to learn, you know. When we moved about on the physical plane in a physical habiliment, we were no wiser than many of your present day teachers. Having groveled around in the darkness of ignorance, after departing the physical coil, our first desire, upon becoming illumined in consciousness, was to return and help man of Earth to understand that man is power and that all power is of God.

How very fortunate it is for us, when we find collaborators whose mortal reasoning is uncluttered from that which man refers to as book learning or mortal logic reasoning. Now, when we say, "book learning," we mean erroneous book learning. For there is a proper intellectual education and improper education. Some type of education leads to a "stiff type of mind." For soul growth and for inner intelligent wisdom, one must be open to new ideas, wider fields of consciousness, a willingness to think. To know the difference between erroneous learning and proper learning, one must quicken the inner consciousness and apply oneself through divine reasoning. Through reflection and proper understanding these erroneous suggestions are then removed when they are presented to man by the now so-called teachers in the schools.

Learn not to be gullible to erroneous teachings, and learn to separate in your thinking the wheat from the chaff. This is what we are interested in doing. We are interested in tearing apart the hidebound teachings of theology, not only of theology, but of all other "ologies" who seek to mislead men of Earth.

Due to the ignorance of the greatest law of life, which is the law of God, man fails to understand his fellowman. The word "Lord" in your Holy Writ should be law, for the Lord of God is, in reality and in truth, the law of God. It is not the physical being as is commonly accepted by the orthodox individual because of the mistranslations.

We are endeavoring to leave with you not one word or thought of negation. It is our desire, as it is your desire, for you to remain free, unencumbered by mortal limitation, and so shall it ever be. When the appearance of adversity besets man, he shall recognize the fact that it is the working out of a debt which has been incurred in a past incarnation. But when it is met in love, tolerance and patience, the debt is well paid and the balance is never found wanting. This is the working out of God's law, divinely so.

We shall continue to speak of love, for love is the power that keeps the universe in motion. As man moves along the path, each adversity he meets is but the balancing of the scale of life, and it cannot prove detrimental. Where it is met with love, it attracts love, and its opposite attracts or begets its own.

We, of the Council, must acquaint man with the fact that the law of God must be lived to the letter and until that time he must continue to struggle with himself. Can the blind lead the blind? Some try, and both fall into the pit together. We are interested only in light, only one light, and that is the light of life. Apply yourself, and you shall never have any regrets because of deception.

Jesus of Nazareth expressed it this way, "By their fruits, ye shall know them." Ye shall. Whenever seeking light and wisdom from some teacher or collaborator, meet him with a blessing. Meet him with a free and open channel of thinking, but always with a blessing, and you shall be able to know and understand whether the wine which comes forth shall be of the sweet grape and not the wine of the decayed, impure or improper grape. We trust that we have been able to make this very clear to you.

You remember the statement, "Test the spirit and see if it is of God." This statement has been misinterpreted by the theologians meaning to test the discarnate spirit. There is to be no fear of discarnate spirit. The spirit referred to that is to be tested, is the spirit which yet has residence on the mortal coil.

Man is incapable of recognizing any master until he first recognizes the master within himself. Man must first come into the consciousness and realization that he is master over all error, and then better shall he behold the masters as they present themselves to him.

May we refer to the statements that you hear around Christmas time, "Peace on Earth; goodwill to men." The proper statement is in this wise, "Peace on Earth toward men of goodwill — God's will." How can a man of ill will recognize peace? How can one who has not reached self-mastery recognize the master who comes in his path? Is this not common sense logic? Is this reasonable or unreasonable to you?

The time has come when with the lowly Galilean you will say, "My kingdom is not of this Earth. Though I am in the world, I am not of it. I and the Father are one." Mind you, the humble Galilean was not referring to himself as he was accepted, as an identity, a physical being with the masses or the throng. When he said, "I," the identity he was referring to was the I AM of God. Therefore, in truth, when he spoke, when he said, "I AM the way...", listen dear hearts, "I AM the way, the truth and the light of life. I AM and you as all men of Earth are a part of the I AM of God."

As physical collaborators, you assume no burden as you continue your Israelitish trek into the fullness of the brightness of the white light of the Great Oversoul. Call it God; call if Cosmic Consciousness; call it what you will; for he who in righteous desire, singles his path to the Father's house, is an Israelite, a traveler along the path of light toward God.

Now some may feel that we are rather partial to that which we call the Holy Writ. What can man understand of that which Gautama Buddha wrote, Confucius wrote, Aristotle wrote, Zoroaster wrote, when they do not understand that with which they are familiar, namely, the Old and the New Testament, called the Holy Writ? All mankind is worthy of salvaging, in spite of his rebellion and rejection of the light. What better way is there to salvage men than by showing them the light of the book that they are now reading and do not understand? Then they can be taken to Buddha, to Confucius, and all the other teachers of ancient age, who are now members of the ancient mystical White Brotherhood. These searchers of truth and light shall then compare the teachings and say within their inner knowing, "Now that I have the understanding of the Holy Writ, I do not find any different in that which heretofore I condemned as null and void."

Would you enjoy telling the story of truth and, in so doing, would you be happy in reaching forth your hand to your fellowman and in truth stating, "Come up higher, you are my brother, you are my sister?" Now, mind you well, we are not advocating proselytizing. How shall you tell the story of truth? Well, as you walk along life's path, you shall continue to meet, as you already have met, those who are footsore and weary of traveling the path of darkness. As shepherds, lovingly lead them.

When the opportunity arises, you will tell them the story of the true light of life. For remember the words of the sage of ancient age, who said, "When the student is ready, the teacher will be provided." Would you become a teacher? Then remember the following:

"Would you know life abundant?
Love doubles for all you give
There is a means no surer,
Than helping someone to live."

And from the pen of another ancient sage fell these words:

"Enjoying each other's good, is heaven begun."

Your dedication shall not become a task, for God imposes upon no man of Earth a task. It shall become a joyous, happy duty. Remember that, "The light which is placed upon a hill lighteth the city wherein is the hill." This shall be an eternal benediction of God, may it grow as you desire it to grow. Love knows no end and Caesar has no power to defeat. What can defeat God's immutable laws of love?

This is our benediction: Go forth, rejoice and prove to the blind of faith, the dumb of faith, that God is. Bless each one, each worker, and as God's eye is on the sparrow, God's eye is upon each one of his beloved collaborators. Go forth, not in physical power alone, but with divine power, your divine power, and you shall find that if you truthfully seek, the door shall remain open because you have zealously knocked. It is granted unto you because in righteousness you have asked. So mote it be, "world without end."

44

CHAPTER THREE

QUICKENING THE MASTER SPIRIT WITHIN

A member of the Council speaks:

In the ever-living presence of God, there is no death.
Memory holds its cherished reflections,
Love is eternal destiny.
Ah love, which never perishes; life which has no end,
God, the ever-living presence
His love does every broken heart mend,
His light makes bright, the places dark
Where man is prone in doubt to wander.
His rod, his staff, they comfort give
His love, the healing waters.

45

With your inner knowing, be attentive. We have one great desire; one great desire have we, and that is to quicken the master spirit within you, so that at all times you shall be aware of peace. Be calm, and no mischief of the mortal mind can cause you to become turbulent. Be at peace, and know that all is well.

We shall never misguide you, have faith. God is no turbulent sea and never shall be. Though the din and confusion of mortal mind be heard on every hand, you shall know nothing but peace. You shall see the lion and the lamb eating straw together and you shall the child playing at the hole of the asp. Though the fire shall come forth from the mouth of the serpent, it shall spell but one word for you: peace.

For truly now and henceforth you can say, "Though I am in the world, I am not of it. I and the Father are one." You shall be the ambassadors of the new order among peoples of the Earth. All peace shall be yours, for you shall learn to make your own peace.

You shall never encounter stormy weather, for you shall create your own weather. Though the clouds in the sky obscure the brightness of the sun, it shall shine in your hearts. You shall never use the attribute of Peter but to deny that of error, for you shall use the regenerated Peter, through faith in God, yourself and your fellowman.

You shall at last come into the perfect realization of the words of the psalmist of old when he said, "He who dwelleth in the secret place of the Most High, shall abide under the shadow of the almighty."

There shall be those who will not agree with you, and that is to be expected. The man or woman who places his foot on the highway of spiritual progress and dares to travel it with no longer a desire to be lost on the road of fundamental superstition, is always criticized and ridiculed. Never has an individual left the beaten path to seek light and truth, but what the understanding in his soul's consciousness has been mistaken for some manner of fanaticism on the part of those who are yet satisfied to be led by those who see the light in no greater brilliance than the ones they are leading.

Never fear to stand for truth. Speak it when it is called forth from you and until that moment, remain silent. How shall you remain silent? In prayerful meditation. Should your path cross with one whom you know is groping in the darkness to the disadvantage of his soul's growth and his physical and material well-being, pray with him.

Man never prays for another; man always prays with another. You may say to me, "How do I know if the one in whom I am interested is praying?" Have you ever had a hope of something good? Have you ever had a heartfelt earnest desire for something good to transpire in your life? If you have, that is a form of prayer. What man-made society calls low, degraded, wretched creatures, as wretched as they may be, at some time or other in their seeming wretchedness, they find themselves saying, "I wish, I trust, I hope, thus and so, thus and so." that is a form of prayer, and all prayers meet.

Remember, dear hearts, though all may not agree as to the orthodox form of prayer, yet even an individual who is steeped in the fundamentals of orthodox theology, prays what to him is an earnest prayer, and all prayers meet.

Now, your prayers uttered in understanding, sent forth to the living God in the tabernacle of the holy of holies, your prayers shall lift the prayers of others. Do not cease to pray.

Should you meet one who is discouraged with life, whether it is by beholding his countenance or by his expressions, if you can do nothing else, reach for his hand, and place your other hand upon his hand. And as you hold it, silently, fervently, and effectually say, "Come up higher, my brother, come up higher, my sister." Silently say, "You are now in the presence of God, and you are now, though mentally distressed in soul and spirit, standing in the tabernacle of the Host, before the table of plenty, and your grief, we place on the golden platter." Do it silently, silently.

A firm handclasp without a word mentioned, a firm handclasp extended and rendered in love is prayer, a most effectual prayer. Remember, a hand extended is expressing outwardly the love and peace of the indwelling God. Never, never fear to clasp a hand.

There is a disastrous superstition among many people and among some ancients, that in accepting the hand of another, there is a possibility of contaminating one's aura. There is only one possible manner in which man's aura may become contaminated, and that is through thinking. Thoughts become living things.

What happens to the countenance when a man is thinking in terms of love? The eyes sparkle and twinkle as the stars at night. The face beams with the radiance of the sun, and the voice sounds as many rippling brooks. That is prayer.

Thoughts of anger? Thoughts of anger are but a perverted form of prayer. Had you ever thought of this? Why does man speak with contempt and viciousness? For the reason that he has been storing up in his thinking, all manner of thoughts contrary to truth. Let the occasion present itself, and that which has been stored up comes forth.

Such are those who are still waiting in the outer court of the holy tabernacle. It is well that you have found them there, for they are desirous of entering the tabernacle. Truly, Paul was right when he said, "Now I see through a glass darkly, but then face to face. When I was a child, I spake as a child, I thought as a child. Now that I am become a man, I have laid aside all childish things." Many are they, who are numbered among adults here on your mundane sphere, who are yet infants in their reasoning.

As messengers sent forth, you have a great duty to perform. You shall enjoy doing it, for the love to perform a duty, never makes of the duty a task. Mind you well, dear hearts, reformation shall not come in an hour, a day or a week, nor a month or a year. Never become disheartened. You shall accomplish much as you travel along life's path.

Should it be so ordained, as it is among some of you, that when you lay aside your earthly coil with no longer a desire to ever again choose another earthly coil, you still serve; there is no death. And to those who are in spiritual truth and are unable to clear the record now, in this present physical journey, they shall be able to choose another body and pick up the threads where they have dropped them here.

Remember, and never forget, though the masses say it is untrue and it does not exist, I say to you without fear of contradiction: man has always tenanted a habiliment of flesh and shall continue to do so, until desire has taken him into the oneness and he becomes numbered with the Council of the ancient mystical White Brotherhood. Unseen to human eye, and from the Council, he shall be able to touch men of Earth, through passing his message on, through those who have reached the secret place of the Most High.

Now, remember, as you go forth to meet groups of people that you are to meet, you are going to render things asunder. You, in turn, shall be torn asunder with criticism, but let it not worry your heart. For there is not a teacher who went forth to teach truth, but that he met someone who did not understand the truth spoken, and viciously condemned the teacher of truth. You understand this, do you not?

Then go forth with the protection and glory of the living God, and you shall not fail. Those who shall condemn you through misunderstanding, what have you done to them? You have implanted a seed which sometime must grow; it shall not perish.

Keep to the principle of truth and never deviate, regardless of circumstances. In so doing, there can be nothing but ultimate success in whatever you attempt. That is true humility. Always remember the word of the Galilean, "Of yourself, mortally so, you do nothing." Neither does any man of Earth; but it is the indwelling Father expressing. How? Through the master spirit within the secret tabernacle in the uppermost part of the brain, the pineal gland, the holy of holies, through the perfect submission of the mortal to the spiritual.

Remember, dear hearts, your physical eyes are the only eyes through which God can now see. Your physical feet are the only feet through which God can walk to carry the message. Your physical hands are the only hands through which God can accept and give (we are now speaking of physical possessions, when we make that statement.) For God gives and receives unto himself, and you are a part of that God.

As you extend your hands and hearts in the love of God to receive, and as you extend your hands in blessing, the indwelling God is extending through your hands and anointing others with the benediction of His eternal blessing. Is this clear to you? God is not far off; God is indwelling. O that man of Earth, at long last, could learn this lesson to be truth.

Truly, then shall the sword of wrath be sheathed, and the lion and the lamb would eat straw together, and the child would play in peace and contentment at the hole of the asp.

In the past, as you call the past, we have heard some of you make this statement, "Why have so many started out on the path to teach, to promote brotherhood, universal brotherhood, and have never brought it to fruition?" That was a desire expressed, whether they were mindful of it or not. That very question placed on the ether waves of time, started action and it came back, back, and back again, into their consciousness.

At last, we, of the Council, were able to make contact with them. Why did they question as to the failure or seeming failure of others? Why did this question arise in your thinking and that of others? For only one reason, dear hearts. Again, as you refer to the past, ages back, you, as they, were singled out by the Council of the ancient mystical White Brotherhood of truth. When the clarion call within your heart intoned its message, they, as you, lovingly responded.

Can love be overlooked? Can graciousness which is expressed without any expectation of reward be disregarded? Ah, nay, nay. It is the expression, beloved ones, of the great white light of the living God. God cannot be denied eternally. He who denied God in yesteryear must, at last, come into full and complete recognition of that which he has denied. He who denies God, in your today, shall live to recognize in truth that which he denies today.

Hence, many of our mundane collaborators and teachers, bear the torch of freedom before the countenance of those who, in yesteryear said, "I have no time for it; it is not so; it cannot be." The torch of truth in the countenance of those of today, shall be reflected in the lives of others, who in the tomorrows, as you understand that term, shall bear the torch of light in their countenance to those who are denying the living God today.

Your labors shall never cease, never, dear hearts. Remember, (if we may use that term in the great scheme of life) rebirth is the salvation of man, and you are playing a most intricate part. Therefore, be faithful, be faithful.

Be mindful, dear hearts, in every life, there comes an hour. In many cases where it has occurred, you sought and sought diligently. Unselfishly, you sought. An earnest desire and an earnest prayer always receive an answer. Like attracts like. It cannot be otherwise, and though, in the past, you may have encountered, from time to time, a deception here and a deception there, you did not forsake your God. That bears its recompense, mind you. So it is no more than truth in the presence of the living God, that, for all of which you bore, and all mankind who walk this path with you, you shall, at last, find what you have been seeking.

Go forth! Spread your seeds of love, for they are falling on fertile soil, and the waters of kindness shall carry them into the soil. All around you, shall you see them spring forth as fields of wheat, and they shall grow, and the heads shall be full. They shall ripen, and you shall go forth and reap the harvest. Many shall there be who shall go forth with you, for you shall not garner the field alone.

CHAPTER FOUR

INVOLUTION OF SPIRIT AND
EVOLUTION OF MATTER

A member of the Brotherhood speaks:

We desire to give all our instruction in simplicity; to make our statements as concise, informative, and instructive as possible. Therefore we endeavor and will continue to endeavor ever to tear aside the veil or curtain of superstition. Man of Earth asks questions for only one reason: because he has become steeped in early superstitions and erroneous teachings. It is for that reason we quite often refer to the Holy Writ with which man in the present era is familiar.

It has been the guideline, and therefore we have ever endeavored to properly interpret for him that which has been superstitiously taught. One of the questions we hear man of Earth ask is this, "If life has always been complete and man and his Creator are one in all aspects of life, why was it necessary for man to make that long trek through the many paths of life, the many incarnations with its many experiences of heartbreak, only to eventually seek his way back through the jungle of illusions, back to the oneness of the Father?"

It is for the reason that man, as man is understood to be, desired to be here. Man did not desire to be or live in imperfection, however. In your Holy Writ, there is the story of the fall of man, do you remember? Also, there is the first murder (if we may use that term) man has recorded: Cain slaying Abel. This is the first recorded murder, and we do not like to use this term as man of Earth does.

Now, of what sum total or composite is man, of that which God created? Out of that which God created, what did God make? You will remember that God created first and then made. And that which God created was good, was it not? Could God have made evil out of that which is good? Some of you might reason that the five senses have misinterpreted the truth, and man lost his way, but how and why do the five senses misinterpret and create that which man today recognizes as evil?

Now, the master Jesus said, "In my Father's house are many mansions." Is this mundane sphere of life that you are living in the only inhabited part in the Father's house? There are many planets that are inhabited and that is truth. Now, all creation was created by God, in the beginning, as well as in the finality. However, as that which God made, out of that which he created, through that which man knows as the process of evolution, the physical form did not keep in rapport with the involution of the soul or spirit. Therefore it became a denser form of the creation of that which man knows as the beginning, and therefore the error took place.

It is this which was referred to in the Scriptures as the "fall of man." It was not because Eve handed Adam an apple. Sometimes it is referred to as the war in heaven. That is well, but ever remember that heaven is a state of consciousness. Some erudite earthly teachers would say that it is at this point the "mind was split." Let us correct such apprehension for the mind was never split, for there is but one mind and that is the mind of God, which is perfect mind, of which man is the perfect part, spiritually so, but, regrettable to say, he is not using it.

Now as that which God made out of that which He created became a denser form of that which man now calls matter; may we repeat, the involution of the soul became retarded and therefore could not radiate its perfection to its fullest extent through that which God made out of that which He created. That was the battle in consciousness.

Man is further deluded to believe, and that is regretable to state, that heaven is a state or place geographically reached, which is not true.

The separation in consciousness would give its appearance as a separation, but in reality, it would be a separation as if in parts or levels, and this is what we are endeavoring to do, to bring all parts or levels back into oneness.

For the master Jesus said, "As in heaven, so in Earth." But the translators said, "As in heaven, so ON Earth." In one of our earlier lessons, we said that the physical body was of the Earth earthy.

Man is not of the three dimensional world. He is of the fourth dimensional world. The fourth dimensional world is the creative power of all that is and of which man is the most intricate part thereof. It is where the union of will and love take place; it is the wedding feast of Cana, where the water was turned into wine; and it made them merry, did it not?

What happens when the involution of the soul keeps in rapport with the evolution of the physical temple? There must then be perfection in the flesh, must there not? It is the turning of the what into what?

In the story of the wedding of Cana, even as it is narrated in the present day Holy Writ, does it not state that as the Galilean turned the water into wine, it created no destruction? They became happy and feasted, did they not?

Therefore then, when man gets back upon the path (if we may use that term) of spiritual realization, of realizing his oneness with the perfect creative power of the universe, the involution of his soul continues and eradicates all imperfection from the flesh temple which has been brought about by that which man calls "error."

And for the want of teaching man something of error, the earlier theological body of the theologians created an entity which they called by name, a devil.

They conceived him with horns, cloven hooves, a tail and a pitchfork, is that right? Then they created a fiery abyss, placed him in the fiery abyss, to reign there forever. That is mythology.

Now, you erase the letter "d" from the word devil, and you have the truth of the existing devil or satanic majesty, if you please. It is "evil", and when man continues to practice evil, it is because he thinks evil first. You cannot practice good or truth until you have first thought it. Neither can you practice anything until you have first thought it. Therefore, the great myth, the great fable of theology, the devil, having walked too far to the edge, because he was angry with God and, in his anger, he fell from heaven to Earth, and then to that place created for him called Hades or Hell; that is all mythology.

It is the descent in consciousness. Now let us reason in this wise: We will accept, for the sake of proof to our statement, that your orthodox theologians are correct in saying that man of Earth can be saved from his sins. We shall accept that temporarily, if that is possible. How is this brought about?

Man listens to the fiery-tongued theologians, the evangelist, the pilgrims of God and their fiery sermons, many of which are based on fear, changes his thinking and therefore, he has become "saved." Is this correct?

Let us come to truth. Does it necessitate a silver-tongued orator, or does it take a fiery-tongued theologian to teach the truth? Is it necessary for the teacher of truth to paint a beautiful picture of heaven with cherubims and seraphims flying about and opposite to it, paint a picture of that which he calls hell, with crackling embers, fire and brimstone?

The teacher of truth paints no such picture! Yet truth teaches man to change his thinking. Thus man, Godman, comes back on the path of involution of the soul (soul's growth in progress), thus evolving the physical temple and bringing it into rapport and unity through the process of evolution. Because of the evolution, the constant and continued growth of the soul brings the flesh temple, "that which God made out of that which God created," back upon the path of that which theology calls righteousness, or right use of mind consciousness. Now is this understandable to you?

There is only one heaven out of which to fall, and that is when man degrades himself in consciousness, mind you that well. For as a man liveth in consciousness, in truth, and in honor, so he shall live in Earth. "As above, so below." As he lives in heaven, in Earth he radiates that to his fellowman. Therefore in our instructions, we have admonished you: never proselytize.

Let your light so shine that your fellowman shall see it. Do not place your light under a bushel. Remember when the Master said, "And I, if I be lifted up, shall draw all mankind to me." He was referring to the ascension of consciousness, into the infinite light, or the I AM.

The one who lives in truth does not find fault with his neighbor or his fellowman. The one who lives in truth is not given over to slander or gossip. The one who lives in truth, when he shares his love and his earthly goods, seeks no glory for it. Thus his fellowman says, "How can they do it? What do they possess that makes of them such very singular individuals?

Thus the neighbor, the fellowman, shall seek to know more about you and your philosophy of life. Thus the so-called hidden mystery of his brother is revealed: humility, humility, humility. The Nazarene knew, for he said, "Let not the right hand know what the left hand doeth." There is another age-old statement, "It is human to err; it is divine to forgive." These are not just coined words; they are definite, positive, accurate, deliberate statements of truth.

As we pass among you, (though we are unseen to human eye) we hear many say, "It is difficult to live as a student or a seeker of truth." Well, it may so appear to some that it is difficult, but beloved, it is not difficult. Remember, all that which you now possess which lends to your comfort, physically speaking, and permits you and others indulgences not enjoyed by many of your fellowman; these comforts and possessions are not just an accumulation of this incarnation; they are the reward of every good you have done as you have crossed life's sands.

That is why individuals have crossed your path. Where you could share and as you have wisely and lovingly shared, you have multiplied your good. In every life's pattern, the bread that is cast upon the waters of life, in love, unselfishly, shall return to the giver or the one who cast the bread. For every good, there is a goodness, and for every goodness, there is another good. And for every good there shall come another goodness. Love begets love; goodness begets goodness.

That action and its equal attraction is the involution of the soul in rapport with the evolution of that which is known as physical body and its environment and circumstance. When the involution of the soul becomes retarded, there is evidence of stagnation of the physical body and its environment and circumstances, for progress shall never spell mortal retrogression. Does this sound reasonable to you?

62

Therefore it is wise for man to remain close to God, for the kingdom of God is in man's consciousness. Where God is, heaven is, and every pure, clean, white, bright, happy, harmonious thought is an angel in heaven.

As man creates angels and sends them forth out into that which man knows as the universe, there shall return to him the manifestation of what he sent out. Remember, "As above, so below. As in heaven, so in Earth."

A prayer of comfort, a prayer of peace, a prayer of love is an angel, dear hearts, a loving protecting angel in God's heaven.

CHAPTER FIVE

FIRST REQUISITE: KNOW GOD AS PRINCIPLE

A member of the Brotherhood speaks:

The ancient mystical White Brotherhood advocates but one principle, the unification of all men of Earth, regardless of religion, color, race or creed. Many are they who understand this principle and the working of the ancient mystical White Brotherhood, for it is no secret.

When man of Earth meets man of Earth for the true spiritual value of man, which is Godman, there is no disappointment. We are endeavoring to help you. Man of Earth must see the Christ-light, the God-light in his fellowman, regardless of the rank, station, or power physically attained. There is only one rank, one power and one prestige in life, and that is spiritual.

Man of Earth cannot believe in two powers or two forces. He cannot believe in God and mammon, for he would love the one and hate the other. There is but one source, the source of God. You may say and be justified in your thinking and saying, "What about those who man meets who may be evil in their thinking?" But, you are not going to meet evil; remember that all men are created equal.

In those who are considered by society as a great evil, there is a part of the Christ power of God, but not so expressing. Remember, those of you whose master spirit is already awakened, and who recognize the goodness of God and the creativeness of God, you behold everyone you see as children of the living God.

Learn to say and learn to mean it, "The Christ in me beholds the Christ in you." Therefore in this manner, you are annihilating that which is referred to as evil. You are beholding the good and meeting the good. To behold is to take hold of and cling to. Remember, the goodness in you cannot become a part of any evil (should it appear so to express), only as you see or express it in your thinking. Man can only become a part of that which he visualizes in his thinking. Therefore as man's mortal thinking becomes pure and elevated, so becomes his subjective thinking and his life's path, which becomes subject to beauty, goodness, to health, spiritual riches, and prosperity.

It is deplorable, but nevertheless true, that mortal education quite frequently retards the expression of spiritual growth. What are we trying to tell you? Go forth to find the radiant principle of the Christ, and you shall bring illumination to those who have not yet found their way.

If the power that man calls God were to discriminate in recognition of mortal achievement, there would be no progress. Go forth, and let all your meetings be with the God-Man or the Christ-Man. The humble soul (as man understands humbleness) radiated the Christ-light to a greater degree than he who walks through marble halls and crystal palaces in that which man calls life, expressing the ego of his temporal personality, strutting with self-importance. Remember, humility accomplishes more than that which swords, bullets, gunpowder, and bombast will ever be able to accomplish.

Mortal man must be reeducated from that which has been destructively perceived by the five physical senses before he can be a pure vessel through which the superconscious, or Godpower, can express. It is not complicated; as the Nazarene said, "As a man thinketh, so is he."

Take yourself a handful of mixed seed and scatter it broadcast over a plot of ground, and it will bring forth blooms of various hues. Each color shall blend with the other until you have a veritable blaze of beauty. Man, supposedly the highest creation of God, is in disagreement one with the other because of the difference of the color of his skin, outward appearances. Man discriminates between one and another, because of what he calls education, degrees of social standing. "Be ye therefore not given over unto appearances, for hath not God written His law in their hearts?"

God does not discriminate, and man is God's creation; when man realizes he is God's creation, he, too, has no discrimination. Remember, it is the Divinity you are seeking in all mankind. Any channel that the Divinity expresses itself through is the lesser of the two. All are worthy of respect, mind you, but the channel is never to be deified. There is only one deity, the deity of God.

"Unto God" let all your errands be, and "Unto God" shall you succeed. When you encounter stray sheep seeking to enter the fold through the doorway (the path of dedication to God through purification of motives), and not over the wall (meaning not wishing to pay the price of the effort and disciplines, nor the price for past disobedience of God's law), it would be needless for we, of the Council, to say, "Be kindly to them." When stray sheep desire to walk the path of light, they are uncomfortable in self-delusion and so seek the light of understanding. Take them by the hand and say, "You are my brother; you are my sister; come up higher, come up higher." Silently or audibly, it

68

matters not, but say it with a smile in your voice and in your countenance.

Religious forms are beginning to wear themselves threadbare and finally come to their native nothingness; man is becoming responsive to the spiritual science. Man must learn to share the truth with others before he can qualify to become a teacher of truth, and he does this by sharing. We are not speaking of earthly accumulations; we are speaking of spiritual knowledge, sharing the understanding of the knowledge you have, sharing the understanding of the wisdom you now have. In sharing it with someone less fortunate than yourself, you will then see the change in your life.

You are seeking spiritual illumination; seek it to share it and enlighten the path of another. The light shed into your path, does it not become an edification to your soul? Be that beacon light to others. We of the Council of the ancient mystical White Brotherhood shall never interfere with man's exercise of his free will. Always feel free to speak and act as your conscience directs.

However, there is a manner in which man should be very cautious in "getting things off his chest", such as that which is established in man's thinking, for man's thoughts are powerful in their own right. But when thoughts are put into action, they gather momentum, and while they may be well understood to the one who mentions them (also the manner in which

69

they are mentioned), they are not always understood with the same weight by the one on whose ears they fall.

Therefore it behooves man, as we have frequently said, to speak with a smile in his voice. We have ears which are no longer physical, and we listen, not only to your audible words of the thoughts you have, but we also look at the thought before it is put into words. From its color, we know its intended purpose.

My dear, beloved collaborators, the day is not too far hence when you shall see the color of thought. When that day dawns, as holding a sieve in your mortal hands, separating wheat from the chaff, as the precious wheat drops through, you shall look at the chaff and say, "Well, this once held the precious kernel of wheat. It is all a part of the pattern and I am not going to discard it. I will make use of even the chaff."

There has never been, and never shall be, a thought so discolored and so distorted but what love can bring it into its proper radiance.

As a student progresses on the path, his thoughts become more powerful, but that power does not affect another until it is delivered in speech. It is that with which we are concerned, for you will remember, and this may be a crude illustration, "Water runs freely over a greased plank." Therefore the plank which is greased with understanding never absorbs the water.

Often, man's understanding is not quite as far advanced as he thinks it is. Often man speaks a trifle hastily and after he has made certain statements, there is a possibility of a season of regret. In making this statement, we are not using a lash, nor do we wish to appear to be chiding. We are interested in but one thing: our purpose is to lead each one of you onto the lighted path. When we can no longer lead you into the light, we stand still and wait until the light becomes recognized, and we know when that has taken place. It is then we again reach forth and say, "Come, you are now ready for the next step."

We do not know the word "discouragement", nor what it means, for we have that to encounter all along the road. Discouragement is of the mortal and we have left that on the mortal plane long ago. Remember, as the Galilean has said, "If I be lifted up, I shall draw all mankind unto me." All mankind, not one, not many, but all mankind.

When some of you passed through the gate which leads to the heart of the great bright light of the universal soul's cosmos, we said to you, "Feed the sheep of the pasture; hold the young lambs to your bosom." Within your soul's consciousness, in silence and sacred reverence, your "yea" was "yea," and unto the mortal your "nay" was "nay," and so it remains, and so it ever shall be.

Let this not appear as strangeness, this that you are about to do, for in the divine plane, there is no strangeness. That which man calls strangeness is but separating the wheat from the chaff in consciousness.

The chaff is not wasted; be mindful of the sieve, for the ripe wheat, as it falls through the mesh, is saved to plant in the fields of the living God, that it may spring forth. Remember, each tiny kernel of wheat brings forth a number of kernels, and each life devoted to the service of God brings forth many souls into the light of truth.

Know God as principle; then ye, too, may be fishers of men. For you are the kernels of wheat in the great field of Christ endeavor. You are the tiny acorns, and remember, the acorn becomes the oak, and on its branches nestle birds that build their nests and raise their young, and beneath its branches the weary wayfarer rests and finds comfort. Each one has his own individual life to live, individual in the heart of God.

You will be mindful we have always endeavored to separate the mixture of personality and the individuality of man. Individuality is God in action; the personality takes on the reflection of environment of the physical. Let us go back to the sieve, the wheat and the chaff. The chaff is never lost.

Orthodox theology speaks of salvation. Let us define the word properly: it is to salvage; it is to establish in truth that which could have been lost through error of interpretation. The pasture of life is filled with sheep, many of which have strayed from the shepherd.

We are evading the word, "must," and supplanting it with the word, "shall." The sheep shall be found. All men are snatched as brands from the burning fire, because mortal man became confused. We lead, and when those we are leading behold the light but dimly, we stand still until we behold the light becoming illumined in the consciousness of those we are desirous of leading. As we have said to you, when we behold your light, we reach forth and say, "Come, you are ready for the next step of revealings."

We, the shepherds of the Father's house, called to you, and through you other sheep have heard the voice of the shepherd. Many prodigal sons have heard through some of you, and they are returning to the Father's house. Strange paths, strange roads, strange avenues, only seemingly so, but the strangeness was but confusion in mortal thinking.

Now, dear hearts, you are no longer limited to the confines of mortal confusion. Have faith and confidence in our leading, for we are not leading you for this moment, for this day, but for that which you have called the tomorrows — tomorrow!

You, as you pass through the gate upon the path leading to the heart center of the great cosmos, you too, will become shepherds in the pasture of God. Truth speaks. One word of truth does greater work, carries greater weight; it is as the tiny kernel of wheat: it multiples. One word of truth grows and it becomes the salvation of man.

The fire of life tempers the steel. The steel must be tempered to serve its purpose. May we help you? You are standing before life's forge, placing your steel, and we, of the Council, shall not see the steel ill-shaped, nor shall we stand by and see you burn yourself while you are being purified by placing your steel in the forge of life. That would not spell reason, would it?

You are not servants, as the word is commonly understood; you are co-workers, young shepherds in the field. In the words of the sage of ancient age of the Far East, " I have traveled life's path many times, and I have yet to find an honest man losing his way on a straight path." Ponder the statement; you are honest, ponder it; you cannot lose your way.

Remember, should there be any loose spokes in the wheel, the blacksmith of life shall fasten them securely to the hub and they shall never become loose again

The word, "Lord" or, "law" of God continues and ever shall continue to be the shepherd of men. When man of Earth understands in his heart's consciousness that God is love, God is truth, God is power, there can be no dismay,no fear, no doubt, no lack of courage. The psalmist has well said, "Yea, though I walk through the valley of the shadow of death, I shall fear no evil." Why is there no lack or fear of evil? The psalmist spoke the word, "For thou art with me, and thy rod and thy staff, they comfort me."

The rod of truth and the staff of understanding have always given and will continue to give comfort. The "Lord or law" established truth and established love of God in man's consciousness. Man's consciousness is but a reflection of man's thinking. As man desires to think Godwise, so man desires to live Godwise. The Christ light, radiant in the consciousness of man, makes all dark ways light and all crooked paths straight.

When, in consciousness, a soul reflects on these truths and will not permit pollution of the clear stream of his life, nor will he accept thoughts of discrepancy or failure, that soul is accepted into the Nehemiah plane of the White Brotherhood, for he has become a constructive worker in the light.

Just as the shining soul of Nehemiah of old, who "hung the gates to the city," the newly entered soul shall claim his birthright in God's love, light and wisdom. It shall walk in the light with the assurance of God, and rebuild in consciousness the walls of his own city of Jerusalem, man's Jerusalem, the Holy City within man's consciousness.

As mankind rises in consciousness, because of its desire to know more of the living God, so each one shall, in turn, become a Nehemiah. The gates shall once again become a protection against the onrush of doubters, those who, in thought, would destroy your Nehemiah consciousness, the builders, the faithful workers of the eternal principle.

When in prayer or meditation, it becomes your desire to seek aid or inspiration from we, of the Council, from our particular sphere of spiritual teachers, or to reach any member on other planes of the heavenly hosts relative to some activity or expression in life, it is then there will be a sincere seeking on the part of the dedicated collaborators who wish honestly to share with others that which is still unwritten, unprinted, undiscovered, unbuilt, or unpainted.

All that is ever necessary is but to visualize us in consciousness, to send out the call, reach up, reach up within and send forth your beam of light within. By using the light which you send forth in prayer or meditation and ascending in consciousness, you will find us there to aid and inspire you.

Remember the law of the magnet: the magnet attracts to itself all that is acceptable to the magnet. And you, dear ones, are going forth in quest of truth, not for yourselves alone, but to share it. Therefore you are the magnet. Always see things with a divine aspect, even though, at times, this seems contrary to mortal conception. That is to be expected.

Being is becoming, becoming is knowing, and knowing is the fullness of wisdom. Dear hearts, always remember, you do not walk alone, and in whatever manner we speak of your true spiritual ability, we have no fear of your ever using this ability selfishly or possessively. We are happy to inform you that you are now penetrating the veil of doubt. All that which has obscured your vision from the fullness of God's knowing is disappearing, as the mist is dissolved by the warmth of the sun's rays. The mist has returned to the oneness of life.

76

We shall never see you wander on barren wastes; that cannot be. "Closer than hands and feet," we remain with you. There can be no barriers, for you do not stand alone. With each pulsation of the blood, as it follows through your physical body, so in consciousness; you will become aware of the vastness in the great pattern of life.

Wherein lies the solution to all that which man calls problematic? In the reality of God, there are no problems. It is only as man hesitates and questions in his thinking does that which man has called a problem arise. God's children were never destined to live in ignorance. Whatever manner of textbook man uses, is but a means to cause him to think. When his thought is constructive, he becomes a part of life's great textbook, wherein lies all wisdom.

When man sincerely understands that he is about the Father's business and shares his Father's business in love, he will not seek rank, station, prestige or power. He will not seek the gilded frame of public fame because of mortal or physical egotism, which ever creates dissension. He will seek but one gilded frame. It is the golden frame created with the gold of love.

We have, in the past, and are endeavoring to ever keep you, dear collaborators, God-conscious. When man fully knows and understands the underlying principle of all life, life will no longer be a mystery. Silence, meditation, quiescence, a continued desire to know further, without argument in mortal reasoning, places him or her in that particular receptive state to receive the enlightenment one is seeking.

The Galilean was correct when he said, "As you sow, so shall you reap." That is the interpretation as you read in your Holy Writ; but in the original it read in this wise, "I am the center of the universe, out of the vast comes nearness."

We have given you a key in some instructions previously given. Remember it always:

> "There is part of the sun in the apple,
> Part of the moon in the rose
> Part of the flaming Pleiades
> In everything that grows.
> Out of the vast comes nearness,
> For the God of love, of which man sings
> Has put a little bit of His heaven
> Into every living thing."

CHAPTER SIX

PURIFICATION — THE PATH
OF REGENERATION

A member of the Brotherhood speaks:

Let there be peace and happiness. Let there be no
confusion in thinking. Let emotionalism be swallowed
up in the victory of understanding. When understanding is accepted and through its acceptance received, it
can only be appropriated in intelligence. Therefore,
there is no room for confusion.

Wisdom begets understanding, and understanding
is intelligence. Then man is no longer confined to the
narrowness of mortal intellect. That has been our goal;
our great aim and purpose is that you, dear ones, see
through one window and behold the great wide vistas

of intelligence. There is but one mind, Godmind, known to many of the Earth plane as superconsciousness.

The soul is the mind power for the duration of each incarnation. That which is known to man as conscious mind or objective mind is receptive to that which the five senses therein record. It is the indwelling place of desire. It is that which records every desire of the five physical senses. It is that which is referred to by man of your teachers as the carnal mind, wherein carnal thinking has its workshop.

During the activity of the day, when the carnal workshop is producing its wares and that portion of the brain is very active, it is there that selfishness, possessiveness, greed, strivings, and tyranny have their residence. When that state, known to man as sleep, manifests itself, then that workshop is quiet. Now, all that it has created during the waking state seeks lodgment in the subjective channels of the brain. You will recall previous instructions in which we likened that which man calls the subjective mind unto a "king" who rules his subjects.

The subjective mind, so known to man, knows only that which the conscious mind, so-called, sends to the subjective or the subconscious mind, so-called. It is there the unfinished business has its residence and becomes a part of the soul. You will be mindful of the statement, "Spirit is willing, but the flesh is weak."

80

The image and likeness of God, which is Godman, has its residence in the superconsciousness, that is, the inner chamber, the "tabernacle of the hosts."

Regardless of what man has written in books, we are endeavoring to share truth with you, that you may no longer walk in darkness. Where, therefore, it is necessary for the regeneration to have its first desire or inception, it needs must be in that which man refers to as the conscious mind or objective mind. It must therefore be objective, dear hearts.

Prayer is the innermost desire of good. When man desires to follow the path of regeneration and purification to build the new foundation for the new pillars of the new Temple of Solomon, the temple of the soul, so that nothing will destroy it ever, it is necessary to first cleanse the channels of communication, so that our messages of inspiration, as we send them to you, are properly received and are crystal clear, free of any distortion or misinterpretation in meaning to your understanding consciousness.

First, one must cleanse and awaken the five physical centers so that the seven spiritual centers may radiate brightly. Prayer is the first step to the fullness of spiritual realization, for remember, "Spirit is ever willing." Spirit does not demand, does not command, spirit is ever willing. Now then, when man becomes fervent in his desire for righteousness in the conscious or objective thinking, he is beginning to cleanse, to

81

purge all that which the conscious or objective mind has accepted in error from the five physical senses.

Steadfast and persistent, without fear, without doubt, the conscious or objective state becomes illumined with desire for good. Now, when that of good leaves the objective thinking, it passes to the subjective and there continues its cleansing of the error which the objective has sent to the subjective. When man of Earth continues along constructive, pure, unselfish ideas, the subjective becomes completely permeated with spiritual, creative records.

It is then, that which man calls superconsciousness of spirit can express its everlasting eternal willingness, then shall come to pass the statement so commonly used in orthodox theology, "the power descends from on high."

Let us mention the magnet, as when holding the magnet beneath a piece of paper or glass upon which are placed bits of metal, which will respond to the attraction of the magnet. As the magnet is moved about, the tiny metal particles form a pattern. Now this pattern could not be formed, regardless of the magnet, unless the tiny metallic particles were there.

Now that which man has learned to call the subjective mind, when it has received thought pictures of love, peace, harmony, contentment, devotion, all that which is in accord with Godman, there is an attraction for the power, the magnet of the superconscious power. The willingness of spirit is then able to manifest, for it cannot manifest until it has that with which to make its manifestation. Therefore in silence, meditation and concentration, any devotion to good, call it what you will, sets in motion in the objective mind that which is the first beginning on the path of the ascension, or the path of regeneration.

We have reasoned with you that man lives by desire, and that is speaking of man's unregenerated desire. Godman lives by desire, yes, but it is always righteous desire, not in the least limited or subjected to that of the five physical senses.

When the subjective mind remains unregenerated and man is separated from the physical coil through what has been called death, when in that state, and when, in time, he desires to return to the physical plane to finish unfinished business, he returns with just those qualities unto which he was subject to by the subjective mind of his former life. They are still a part of his desire pattern.

Now this, we are aware, is in direct contradiction to much of which man of Earth today understands, but when this law is understood, man shall be mindful how he weaves the daily portion of life's pattern allotted him to weave through his living.

Hence, the age-old statement, "As you sow, so shall you reap," until by continued mistakes, pain and suffering, he learns the lesson.

Why pain? Why suffering? Why want? Why lack? Why limitation? Are they the result of disobedience in

83

some incarnation? Nay, nay, nay! It is an accumulation of repeated unfinished business of many lives and many incarnations, the rejection of facing the responsibilities of life and the principle of truth.

It therefore behooves man to seek a righteous path. Fear, doubt, and emotionalism are contributing factors, in your everyday terminology. They are the contributing factors to an unsound subjective intellectual picture, making it difficult, thought not impossible, for intelligence to permeate the intellect. May we repeat, as we have oftentimes stated, mortally, man is a weakling; spiritually he is a giant.

Every fragment of doubt, fear, and superstition shall be removed from the subjective chamber, lest they continue to retard progress. Eventually, that which man of Earth has learned to call death shall be annihilated, for there is no death.

Can man of Earth so live life's pattern that it is unnecessary to return and claim another physical vehicle? Our answer is yes! Yes, yes, yes! But he shall pass through the regeneration. When mortal man will use for himself that which he suggests to his fellowman to use, he will become a good teacher of truth, first to himself.

In one of our previous instructions, we said, "Man can share with his fellowman only that which he possesses. And have we not also stated "professing is not possessing?" When one really possesses the radiance of spirit, it illumines the countenance, and his fellowman will say, "What has he, what has she, which I do not possess?" For the "eyes shone forth as stars in the firmament, and behold, the countenance thereof was radiant as alabaster, and the feet (understanding) were as gold, and the raiment (aura) white as snow."

When the woman whose physical habiliment was tortured with an issue of blood for many years, and she had spent her worldly possessions and yet the issue of blood remained, "She touched the hem of the garment."

Does the universe have an aura? Yes! Do they who dwell in the universe have an aura? Yes! Do nations have an aura? Yes! Do cities have an aura? Yes! Do races have an aura? Yes! Everything that lives has an aura, dear hearts. So, the woman who had reached forth touched the "hem of the garment," the garment she touched clothed a physical habiliment and that physical habiliment clothed a soul, and that soul was subject to but one power, the oneness of being. Therefore there was but one aura in that garment, the aura of peace, love, healing, dear hearts.

You will remember the remaining part of the narrative. The Nazarene saw her not; neither did she behold the countenance of the Nazarene, and yet he said, "What manner of man hath touched me?" He was informed by the disciples that none had, unaware that the woman had touched the garment. The Nazarene said, "Verily, for this moment I felt a virtue leave me."

What a beautiful symbology man has here: the Nazarene is the embodiment of the Christ Consciousness, as all mankind is the embodiment of the Christ Consciousness. The twelve disciples surrounding the Nazarene, symbolizing in man of Earth the beautiful thought pictures, the twelve powers of man spiritually expressed, the thoughts of righteousness expressed, sent to the subjective chamber, giving protection to man physically and spiritually.

What symbology bears the press of the throng? The disciples were within the protecting circle, mind you. The throng was seeking, were they not? Among their number were many who were anxious to be healed of body, symbolizing the first steps in desire for regeneration. All this was symbolized in the consciousness of the woman. Mind you, she did not let doubt interfere. She did not let fear interfere. She reached through the throng, the press of the crowd with but one desire in objective consciousness, one desire to reach the Master.

That part of the aura which became permeated with righteousness, blended with the aura of the Master Jesus. Her divine self, her master in consciousness, became awakened and the issue of blood ceased. The Galilean knew when he said, "Arise, take up thy cross and follow me." Not follow him as the man Jesus; he did not mean this, but following the Christ light of the inner Godman.

86

When the innate, persistent, unmoved, fervent desire remains steadfast in the objective consciousness, there can be no subjects in the subconscious chamber to misguide the subjects of the flesh habiliment.

Godman comes into his rightful heritage and rules on the throne of authority, on the seven spiritual centers, radiating their spiritual light and power through the etheric body, purifying and spiritualizing the physical centers and the pillars of the Temple of Solomon.

In the spine are two central nerves known to man of Earth as the great ganglia or ganglionic system of nerves. They are referred to in your Holy Writ, as well as in the teachings of free and accepted Masonry, as Boaz and Jachin (1 Kings 7:21), which were given by Solomon to Hiram of Abif in recompense for his services in the construction of the temple.

In the lower part of the spine of the human or physical habiliment, is a portion of gray matter, similar in construction to the gray matter of which the brain is made. In the front, or in the region of the navel, is likewise a similar substance of gray matter.

Man does his thinking in that region of the abdomen, right in back of the navel, and over a fine network of nerves its messages are sent and reach the substance in the lower part of the spine, known as the kundalini center. That center acts as your present day telegrapher's key and sends the messages up the ganglionic system of nerves to the brain. This is referred to in your Holy Writ, in the book of Revelation, as "the twelve branches of the tree." Now the messages that reach the various cell centers of the brain are sent through the physical body to each intelligence or nerve center. Through the physical habiliment are trillions of minute nerve centers, intelligences in their own right. They shall accept whatever message is sent to them and respond in accordance to that message. Therefore, if they receive a message of distress, mortally so, that is the only message they can respond to. But if they receive a message of constructive or affirmative structure, that is the message they shall respond to.

Therefore it behooves man at all times to think in an affirmative manner, even though he is becoming interested in that which is foreign or strange to him. It is unwise for him to become destructively critical; for in truth, all things are possible.

Remember always, these pillars keep in perfect order the physical structure of the Temple of Solomon, the temple of the soul. Likewise, in your Holy Writ, in the book of Revelation 22:2, you will read, "The branches and the leaves were given unto the nation (which means mankind) for the healing," and healing is constructive. Therefore all thoughts should be constructive and not in the leastwise negative.

It is unwise for man to say, "I do not know," or, "I am not interested," or, "I do not care." All ideas are worthy of consideration, for all constructive ideas come from the vastness or from the constructive source or seat which man has learned to call God.

God is not man, as man beholds himself. God is power, God is truth, God is love; and that which teaches man the power of God, the love of God, and the truth of God is worthy of man's consideration and acceptance regardless of the channel through which it comes.

The Nazarene said, "Unto him who keepeth my law, I shall give unto him for an inheritance, the heathen." In your present interpretation, the heathen is understood as one who is without understanding or learning, and that is untrue. When Jesus made that utterance, the heathen were considered to be quiescence, humility, and acceptance. Therefore the Nazarene was expediently wise, when he said, "To inherit that which promulgates truth, is to inherit the power or the understanding of the power that promotes life."

Therefore the Temple of Solomon becomes as substantial as man in his thinking causes it to be. Now mind you well, "As man thinketh in his heart, so is he." And the heart that the Galilean referred to was the brain; that is the heart of man, for each part and particle of the physical habiliment, or the Temple of Solomon, responds to man's thinking as it passes back and forth through the pillars of the temple, known as the ganglionic system of nerves.

Has it ever occurred to you that upon hearing some distressing news, you have had the experience of a weak, nauseating feeling in the region of the navel? Or if you have become startled over some sudden news which you have accepted in a negative manner? That is because that center has rebelled against the negation or physical weakness that man experiences with a psychic reaction.

Man so often complains, physically, of a pain across the small of his back and attributes it to some physical weakness. That is not true. It is that center known as the kundalinic center rejecting that which is untrue and endeavoring to separate the wheat from the chaff, so that the message passed up to the brain, through the pillars of the temple, reaches the twelve cranial nerves uncontaminated from error and sends to the cell structure of the brain, the true and uncontaminated message of life, peace, power, and plenty. We trust you shall mentally digest and assimilate this information. Many have misunderstood much of what they have read in books about the construction of the ganglionic system of nerves, and they will not be in agreement, perhaps, with that which we are stating; however, with that we are not in the leastwise concerned.

It is our endeavor to lead man of Earth, "from the unreal to the real, from darkness into light, from death unto life, from mortality to immortality: life eternal." There is but one life for man to live and that life is continuous, regardless of that which has been spoken of, mentioned or written about down through the centuries, as you reckon time. That life is allotted into portions; those portions are known as rebirth; so it behooves man in his thinking to set his house in order.

Let us be clearly understood. It is not God's decree or dictum that man shall reincarnate or be born again. As man is now experiencing life in his present physical temple, he can make this adjustment by following the path of regeneration and rising in consciousness, thus making it unnecessary to choose another physical body in which to correct his error or pay his debt.

As man lives in each physical body, he incurs a debt or creates the thought desire which shall bring him back in another physical tenement or another Temple of Solomon.

You will remember the narrative of the wall of Jerusalem being repaired? That is what rebirth means to man: returning to repair the walls of Jerusalem, and that repair can be accomplished in the present incarnation by creating no further error in thinking.

Let man's thought be pure and righteous, which is right and uncontaminated by the antiquity of race consciousness. Separate the wheat from the chaff, and let your wheat be milled into a perfect loaf leavened with the leaven of righteous understanding, that you may feast upon that which spells out freedom and liberty.

The Nazarene likewise said, "By their fruits shall ye know them." (Matt. 7:20) The apple tree bears apples, not a plum or a pear. Each tree, its own fruit, so the Galilean was expediently wise when he made that statement, "By their fruits, shall ye know them."

Mortal man is inclined or prone to live a life or expression of pretense. Outwardly, he may manifest righteously and inwardly be filled with contempt. Now we do not mean to be destructively critical, but you have found that to be so, and man's inward thinking or his inward emotion never becomes so enshrouded by the outer pretense that it absolves him from creating an error within himself.

First, man shall be true to himself, and then he shall be true to his fellowman; for by being true to himself, he is true to his God, and the proper message, the affirmative message is passing back and forth through the great pillars of the Temple of Solomon and reaching the cells in the brain and putting all in righteous or rightful order.

CHAPTER SEVEN

THE ALCHEMY OF DIVINE THINKING
also
ANCIENT SYMBOLS

One of the Brotherhood speaks:

> Your summer has fled and the autumn comes,
> Revealing the beauty of the summer spent.
> Nature begins its quiet sleep, but to recreate,
> There is no death and nothing is lost;
> Life is eternal.

In the quiescence of this moment, contemplate the beauty of your life. Many summers have you seen and many autumns, too. All of beauty is yours. The sun has spent its day with you. The mantle of night in its sweet caress enfolds you and you rest.

93

It is always a blessed privilege to share with you the precious truths of life and as you well understand, that which man has learned to call error is but an illusion and is not of God. God is the perfect being, the perfect principle of life.

As we have previously mentioned, God becomes personalized, the manner in which man of Earth in his desire consciousness seeks to serve and spiritually share.

As you well know, and have found so to be, there is but one power and one presence in the universe, God, the good. As man desires so to grow in this presence, the greater becomes the realization. Never fear that which is as yet seemingly unknown to you. It shall never be seen by mortal sight. Your mortal or physical eye sees because of the spiritual light of God.

God is power, and for man to deny that truth, causes that to take place which he recognizes as infirmity. Always remember, dear hearts, you are the image and likeness of God, spiritually so. Spiritually, you are birthless, ageless and deathless. When this truth continues to abide in conscious recognition, the illusion of its opposite can never represent any recognition.

In truth, man of Earth has no mind, he is mind, and in that which man recognizes as a brain, he has the divine faculty of thinking. As he thinks, so shall he be.

What we are about to say are not idle words, "As a man thinketh in his heart, so is he." The heart of man is the kingdom of God within, and it is found in the uppermost part of the brain. The Psalmist knew this, and he referred to it as the "secret place of the Most High." In your Holy Writ, you read of it as "the throne seat of God." This we have spoken of previously.

There are myriad cells throughout the physical body, and, in the brain, there are likewise millions of cells. Each cell, both in the brain and the body, are intelligences in their own right. Then, when the cells in the brain are given the message of life, light, and truth, these messages are communicated immediately to the cells in the body.

Where the cells in the brain have been fed destructive thoughts formerly, such as, "I can't do this," and, "I am all in, I do not have the strength, I do not know how," etc., the body has become weakened and ill. Now that the constructive thoughts are replacing those formerly sent, they begin to awaken the cells of the body unto righteousness (right use of the God force) and the body responds.

Man shall become of greater concern with his spiritual body, for it is the spiritual body where man has his residence. As in thought, he desires that which is life, light and power, so he permeates the spiritual body, and the spiritual body, in turn, radiates that perfection to the physical or mortal habiliment. Thus when man recognizes God in the true sense, there can be no failure or sickness of the physical body.

When man recognizes his oneness with God, with the "holy of holies," meaning perfection of pure being, and being its likeness in its image or mind, or its likeness, meaning one with, having no separation from the source of the absolute pure being, then he becomes what is known to man of Earth as an "overcomer."

You will experience and find that there is no lack, no want, and the greatest recognition of God is to continually state or affirm, "I am at peace. I am abundant power. I am strong and perfect in being." For, you will remember, when Moses received the command from God to lead the people from the bondage of pharoah, he said to God, "Whom shall I say has sent me?" and the voice within answered, "Thou shalt say, 'I AM hath sent me.'"

I AM is the name of God. Spiritually, man knows no limitation, for there is no separation in God. There cannot be. Should there come across your path one whom you, out of spiritual love, desire to help, and you find his understanding of God's law is less fortunate than yourself, you shall silently command, in silence (it shall be sufficient), "You are a child of the living God; you are one with spiritual perfection." As God's eyes are too pure to behold iniquity, you therefore behold only that which is God-created, that which is eternally perfect.

You will remember when the man possessed of demons stood before the Galilean. What were the demons or the devils that the Galilean cast forth from the man's thoughts which were contrary to oneness with God? As the story relates, the demons spoke to the Galilean and said, "You are the Christ of God; we will have nothing to do with you."

The darkness created by destructive thinking (demons in thought) began to vanish, light began to descend and as the destructive thinking began to vanish, the man possessed of demons was healed.

The Galilean said, "Unto him who passes through the regeneration, I shall give unto him power to sit upon 12 thrones, ruling the 12 tribes of Israel." Now unto him who is Israelitish in his thinking, who is in quest of spiritual liberation, that one becomes a Moses unto himself, a deliverer and emancipator, and seeks the land of Cana or the land of righteous plenty. He is using the divine mind of light and wisdom.

In your Holy Writ, you will read the statement, "letting your light so shine." The mortal or physical eye of your fellowman, may never see the beauty of your aura, but long before they have ascended to the heights enabling them to behold this beauty, spiritually so, it shall be felt.

Men's auras mingle, you know, one with the other. When you are in the presence of another, and you feel weakened or depressed, and you are desirous of freeing yourself from that presence, it is because your aura has become spiritualized, that it can find no recognition in the aura of the one in whose presence you may be at the moment.

But when your auras mingle and you are at peace and happy, you say to yourself, "I just cannot wait until I meet them again." This assures you of a spiritual radiation from the aura of the one in whose presence you have been. "Let your light so shine." Likewise the statement, "And I, if I be lifted up, shall draw all mankind unto me."

The Nazarene was not speaking of himself; he was referring to the I AM of God, for the masses recognized him as Jesus of Nazareth, but the I AM of God is the complete reflection of the Presence, the one Presence, the one power of the universe, omnipotent, omniscient, omnipresent.

Have no fear to say, "I shall succeed; I can do it," for it is God's desire for all his children to succeed. The man or woman of Earth, who succeeds and continues in success, is the man or woman who has received his success from the I AM consciousness of God.

This consciousness of God is quite often affectionately and commonly recognized and expressed as divine mind. Man spiritually is a divine creation and ever shall be. Man is a giant, spiritually; mortally, he may be a weakling, but spiritually, nothing is impossible for him to accomplish. Have no fear to say, "I am all love; I am all power; I am all that which God so desires me to be." Thus the impersonal God becomes personalized.

When your physical voice speaks in terms of love, you are speaking with the mouth of God. When your physical eyes beam with happiness and you behold your fellowman in equal spiritual measure, one with the other, you are then seeing with the eyes of God. When you reach forth in fond embrace, you are extending the hands of God. For remember, you are the incarnate image of the one living God. Not a living God, but the one living God, for there is but one God. Thus for you to say a living God is to infer that there are many living Gods.

Let the meditations of your heart be ever of God, for remember, the heart of man is in his thinking, and when the meditations of your heart are God-wise, the words of your lips shall be likewise. For man cannot utter a word until he has first thought it. Therefore may we repeat, "May the meditations of my heart and the words of my lips ever be unto Thee, O Jehovah."

With that affirmation in your thinking, that which man has considered obstacles shall soon pass and his fellowman shall no longer be boresome or tiresome to him, for he shall have accepted his fellowman, regardless of his color or creed, rank, prestige or power. He shall be able to say in truth, "The Christ (consciousness of goodness) in me beholds the Christ in you. The Christ (purity of love and truth) in me greets the Christ in you."

To those of you who are interested in that which affectionately or commonly is referred to as metaphysical healing, never see your fellowman or his physical body in any other state than the state of perfection.

There are, in your mundane sphere, certain schools of thought which teach affirmations and denials. We are familiar with them and do not destructively criticize their teachings, but may we leave these words of truth with you? To deny distress is to acknowledge its existence, is it not so? Therefore you may be justified to ask this question, "When man, in his ignorance of thinking, has caused his physical body to become uncomfortable, what shall we do?"

Our answer to you, dear hearts, is this. Remember the words of the supreme teacher of the ancient mystical White Brotherhood. When he stood before the tomb of Lazarus, his first statement was, "Father, I thank thee that Lazarus liveth." And then he said, "Lazarus, come forth!" In expressing affirmations of truth, either silently or otherwise, it never becomes necessary for the expression of denials, for truth has overcome all that needs to be overcome.

Upon the scroll of thy inner vision, ye shall behold these words, "Now abideth faith, hope, and love, but the greatest of these is love." Faith, what is faith? It is no greater, no less, than trust. Trust in what? Trust in whom? Trust in God. Hope, what is hope? It is nothing greater, nothing less, than the realization that everything is possible with the law of God. For there cannot be one among you, who having passed along the edge of what appeared to be an impending disaster, has not experienced the lifting up, the transformation, the renewing. Surely, you have had revealings of all that which has come to pass.

When the hour has come and seemingly been the darkest, this help has come because of no particular physical effort and without the assistance of those you have learned to call men and women. Where has it come from? It came from the indwelling divine mind: God.

Faith, trust, hope, revelation, love, and the last, love, is no greater, no less than honor. How can man dishonor God? You will remember God is both masculine and feminine. Therefore the ancient sage and prophet said, "Honor thy father and mother." It is not complicated and it is not a mystery: only as man, either in his lack of desire to understand, or his willful rejection, places himself on what you have learned to call a quandary or a mysterious nonreceptive state of thinking.

Man has spoken of becoming conscience-stricken. That is impossible without first having had some awareness of his higher self, either a fragmentary understanding, or premonition of the results of rejection of the higher self. Conscience is the foster child of consciousness.

Why are we speaking to you in this manner? We love you and we see the lights of your aura and know

101

that the desire of your heart is to become as pillars of a new temple, as candles in the golden candlestick of God's altar. Your light shall shine and burn only as you permit it to burn, to reveal to others through faith, hope, and love.

The greater one's sincerity becomes in his or her quest to behold the fullness thereof, the radiance thereof, to behold the heart, the center of the great white light of the Universal Soul, the less he or she becomes involved in the throes of physical emotion.

In keeping with and true to our promise, we shall ever be at hand, as close if not closer than the hair of your head. You call, we shall answer.

Give consideration and careful attention in thought to what we have spoken of; digest it, and you will find a pattern of conduct. This information has been given for the reason that it has not been our intention, nor shall it ever be, to inflict the least particle of unconcern to the intelligence you now possess.

It has not been too far distant when we endeavored to separate the mixture of individuality and personality. Personality is the child of intellect. Individuality is the mother and father of intelligence. It is God in action. Intelligence is the only mind man of Earth shall ever know anything about. It is divine and eternal. Therefore in your intellectual reasoning, which can savor of misinterpretations of the five physical senses, it behooves man to consider the manner in which he conducts himself in his thinking. Intellect passes through the endless process of regeneration. Remember, intellect reflects, not merely reflects the personality, but it also reflects race consciousness. Therefore intellect must make its ascent and meet intelligence, which is God.

The Chinese would have been the most powerful nation in the world, had it not been that they took into too great a consideration the dynasties from which they sprang forth. "We are from the house of Ming." "We are from the house of Wong." "We are from the house of Moy." "We are from the house of Laong." They forgot the truth that their Confucius and Buddha taught. Confucius and Buddha said, "You are supreme intelligence."

If Buddha and Confucius never did one mite of good, (which they did) they established the greatest code of moral ethics ever left to human kind. The Galilean clarifies their code of moral ethics with the great white light of the oversoul.

Race consciousness, humbly bowing before ancestry, became the death knell, as it were, of the Chinese. In the Scripture, you will read a verse in this wise, "The dragon shall give the beast its power." (Rev.13:2) And the dragon shall, for the dragon shall come into its rightful possession. When you see "flame of light" depicting the emanation from the dragon's mouth, it is not destructive; it is the flame of purification.

Remember, not all animals are beasts, nor are all beasts animals. "The dragon shall give the beast its power." When it is the golden serpent of wisdom, then only will the "beast" (the mortal intellect) be cleansed with the purification of the spiritual flame. Wisdom — you possess it — use it, and it shall have a greater realization for you as you raise your intellect to meet intelligence, as a true alchemist of God, turning base thinking into the gold, noble thinking of pure wisdom.

Intelligence is not the destructive serpent; it is the flame of purification. It is the light which leads man out of the darkness, the wilderness of mortal intellect into the freedom of God's unfailing light. Do not worry about that which your fellowman believes in. Never ask him to accept what you have to offer. Remember, all man is born of free will. Therefore we have stated many times: No proselytizing. Share that which you understand and know. Share it only when it is sought and when you feel it is necessary. You are now in life's laboratory; a true chosen and bidden alchemist are you when you rise in intellect, which is knowledge, and tap the universal storehouse of wisdom, which is divine mind, God in action.

You shall then prove to your predecessors that they who denied God, denied the origin of that which they were seeking, for the reason that their test tubes, which is their mortal reasoning, failed. "Faith, hope, love, these three, but the greatest of these is love."

As the bud which breaks forth and reveals the beauty within its heart is unknown to man until it blooms or blossoms, so you shall burst forth in the fullness of spiritual consciousness. The man who stands on his own two feet and swings his own body, that is the man or woman we are looking for, for that man or woman is then coming closer to the real man or God-man, which you are in truth.

Love is power and when it is unselfishly shared, never causes a moment of regret. There is nothing in nature that stands still, for God is active principle; God is radiant intelligence. Being is becoming, becoming is knowing, knowing becomes understanding, and understanding begets intelligence.

What is "self-realization," a term often used on Earth? Man is self-realized when the soul realizes that man is one with God, and conducts himself in all his experiences in conformity with that realization. There can be no other self-realization; God and man are one.

There are many ancient symbols which are recognized as having the same eternal, cosmic meaning wherever they may be found. Among them, there is the circle, symbolizing eternity; also, the sun or light. Then there is the crescent moon, symbolizing a sign of newness among men of Earth. The triangle indicates the triune principle of life. The crown symbolizes the glory of God made manifest as victory in truth. The cross symbolizes the resurrection and ascension in consciousness.

Long ages past, David, the shepherd boy, while watching the stars, conceived of the truth that God and man were one, spiritually speaking. He was divinely inspired to perceive that the triune principle of life was expressed in spirit and also in material form. These two triangles are the spiritual triangle pointing upward, and the physical triangle pointing down. He symbolized the realization by interlacing the two triangles, the one triangle pointing upward to God and the other triangle pointing down to Earth, the six-pointed star, symbolizing the oneness of God and man. Meditate on the true meaning of these interlaced triangles; learn the lesson well and you shall be self-realized in the oneness of God.

Let us now consider the six-pointed star, the two triangles and what they represent in the physical body. The triangle pointing down is in the direction of the seat of the sun, or the solar plexus. It is here that man begins his rise, his ascent in consciousness. In the seat of the sun is the fire of the universe that burns up all error. The upper cross point of the triangle governs the heart and the lungs.

In the triangle which points upward, the apex points to the sacred and secret place of the Most High, where man eventually resides in his awakened state. The two lower points cover the liver and the spleen. We are pointing out the six prominent powers of the physical body. When these six stations, or centers, are properly functioning, they are devoid of the clutter of emotionalism.

The chemistry of the physical body is in perfect balance, and that which man calls disease, or any other form of discomfort, is unknown to the physical body.

When the chemistry of the physical body is imbalanced, the waters of life which man calls the bloodstream become overtaxed through the contamination and disturbed thinking. Nature does not quit; nature does not take a holiday. Nature asks for help and that which has been in the process of making over what man calls days, weeks, months, and perhaps years, is not always overcome in the twinkling of an eye.

Therefore it behooves man never to become part of outward appearances when he desires to help his fellowman. True as the words were written, so true they are: thoughts become things.

Just as Jesus of Nazareth, an elder brother of all mankind, is a fellowman to every man who seeks this understanding of life and light, let man not reject it, regardless of where he finds it. Let man be thankful for that light. "The Father and I are one." That thought held in supreme consciousness shall be the tinder that shall set aflame the light of self-realization.

You are now alchemists, mental alchemists. You shall turn the unreal into the real, not only in one manner, but in many; tolerance is priceless. You will find it a handmaiden with love. To be truthful, it is born from the womb of love. We love you; we love you, and it is ever our aim and purpose to lead you bit by bit, step by step. Never let us be accused of causing you mental indigestion. Remember, that which man perceives through his five senses endows him with mortal intellect.

In the speaking of many words and the making of many books, there is the greatest fallacy; therefore the teacher puts acceptable words into being. Intellectual knowledge becomes wisdom when properly applied, when properly understood. When man of Earth ascends in consciousness, his knowledge becomes wisdom, for knowledge is clarified with wisdom. When understanding comes, then theories become facts; until understanding dawns, theories are mere intellectual knowledge. But when understanding dawns, then theories become facts and facts are undeniable. It is wisdom to always walk in the light.

Remember and never forget, the door to the chamber of silence is never closed. There is no mundane power in that which man has learned to call evil, which can close the door to the chamber of silence. In the chamber of silence is the vastness of pure being. Mortal emotion knows no silence. Silence is spiritual adoration unto the living God.

The acorn knows it will be an acorn when planted and a father to a tree some day; the pumpkin knows it will never be a squash; and the carrot seed knows it will never become an apple or a plum, for the seed is imbued with divine mind, and knows from whence it came and whither it is going.

Soon your ground will be covered with snow and ice and the beautiful rose bushes will have gone to sleep; but in the spring, as you understand the seasons, the rays of the sun will kiss the ground and the rose bush shall leaf and the buds shall unfold. Their beauty and perfume shall say to man, "God lives and all is well."

The key to remember:

> There is a part of the sun in the apple,
> Part of the moon in the rose,
> Part of the flaming Pleiades
> In everything that grows.
> Out of the vast comes nearness,
> For the God of love,
> Of which man sings,
> Has put a little bit of His heaven
> Into every living thing.

Dear hearts, everything there is expresses life; as inanimate as it may appear to be, it expresses life, the life of God in action. So let your light shine through using the divine mind to grow, to bless others as well as yourself. There is but one growth and that is spiritual; therefore God first, last, and eternal.

There is only one word that expresses spiritual progress: love. He who loveth is bourn of God, not merely born of God, but lifted, sustained, conveyed and transported. It is for that reason that love, the greatest power in the universe, love, expresses God. When man uses or expresses love and wisdom in all his efforts, in his thoughts, words and deeds, he is working in the laboratory of his life and is a true alchemist using the true elements of God, and showing reverence to the eternal, ancient symbols of the universe all about him.

CHAPTER EIGHT

YOUR AURA — THE SHIELD OF PROTECTION

One of the Brotherhood speaks:

You must learn the accomplishment of loving thoughts, loving thinking. The Galilean healed with love, you know, and the same power flows today. It is a mighty force.

Love is the light which lights every dark path; love is the power that straightens every crooked road; love is that God-in-action which eradicates from every nook and cranny of life whatever has sought lodgment there to disturb.

Love, love, love, use it bountifully. The more you use, the more you shall have to use. You shall have every evidence round about you of that which you have to this hour accomplished through love, love, love, love, for it is that part that God has placed of Himself into every living thing.

Yes, God placed His love; God does not deny love. Man, in his limited mortal understanding, denies it, and denying it, he deprives himself of a priceless treasure. The Galilean said, "Where your heart is, there your treasure lies." The greatest treasure in life, dear hearts, is love. You cannot talk of it enough; you cannot sing of it enough, and you cannot hear of it enough.

Love is a magnet; it never draws the opposite to itself. Remember that and when you have that rooted and grounded in your consciousness, you have discovered the greatest secret in life.

Love never attracts hate; it cannot. Love never attracts tyranny; it cannot. Love is the fullness of light. It is full of life. Love is that power which caused the walls of Jericho to fall. Read that narrative. It bespeaks a spiritual truth as do all other narratives in that book which man has called the book of mysteries.

Love banishes fear. Love annihilates hate. Love destroys tyranny and deception. The man or woman who loves that which he is engaged in doing, performs a duty and that duty never becomes a task. For love knows no task.

You admire the rainbow, do you not? As you see it in the sky, it forms an arc. It is not just an arc, however; it is ovoid in its shape. With the physical eyes, you see but that portion of the circle which, to your vision, appears as an arc of light.

Man's aura envelops his physical body and as the rainbow, it is ovoid in shape. Man's physical body, in reality, is ovoid, mind you that well.

Your aura contains every color in the spectrum of the sun. Oh, if man could but see his aura, when he is thinking unkindly or speaking rash, harsh, unkind words. If he could but see the change that takes place in the spectrum of his aura, he would never again think an angry thought, let alone speak in anger.

What do you think took place when the great Buddha rejected the vilification of the one who sought to slander him? He thought in love. Therefore he kept the brilliance of his aura; he maintained peace and the tranquility of God; and he refused to accept the vilification of his persecutor. That which his persecutor offered him could not penetrate Buddha's aura and cause any unpleasantness in the physical structure of Buddha.

Remember, dear hearts of God, your aura extends about your body as far as you can stretch your hands or your arms. In periods of deep meditation, it extends twice as far and farther. When you are happy and are truthfully in harmony with your fellowman, without enmity, your aura extends quite some distance, just as it is elevated in a spiritual manner through the state of meditation.

113

Man's aura is his shield of protection. Remember, man's aura is man's protection. When, through man's thinking, the colors are kept crystal clear and radiate brightly, man can walk through the abyss of Hades and fear no evil.

Let he who is living the life of a mystic live in the protection of his aura. In mortal thinking, when one does not accept the negativeness of another, the aura of the mystic remains his spiritual fortress. That is the shield and buckler of which the psalmist wrote.

The psalmist knew this when he said, "Yea, though I walk through the valley of the shadow of death, I shall fear no evil, for Thou art with me (the immutable Law of Love). Thy rod and thy staff, they comfort me." If man of Earth were to have the proper understanding of that which he recognizes as the scripture, he would no longer wallow in the pit, the slime, or the grime of fear. He would not be in ignorance of God's truth.

It is unfortunate that the inspirations of the ancient prophets have been misinterpreted. Listen carefully, dear hearts. You enter the silence of meditation for inspiration, do you not? And you receive inspiration quite frequently? So it was with the prophets of old. They were spiritual beings clothed in habiliment of flesh, and they were led by the great teachers of the ancient mystical White Brotherhood, after the Order of Melchizedek.

114

Those who have chosen to follow will have every reason to rejoice that they have been called. For our love and spiritual affection for them becomes greater and greater, for the reason that they have been tolerant and endeavoring to the best of their ability to so order their way along life's path. Also, because they will never become beset with the erroneous desires to resort to subterfuge, thus misusing that power of which they are an incarnate expression, the power of God.

"Let there be peace, and let it begin with me" Let your thoughts ever be thus and should you perchance become alerted to the deception of others, never let it become a part of you. Keep your aura bright, crystal clear, so that you will attract from the aura of others only that which is as clear as your own aura.

When you see an overcast countenance in others, smile! When you see a distorted, emaciated physical form in others, with your inner eye, see it straight, strong, and stalwart. When you see the uncertain step, see it move with steadiness within the inner recess of your soul's consciousness. Then happiness shall be one of your greatest rewards.

Remember, that which you are preparing to do requires patience and tolerance, and there shall be no negative statement, no "hopes" or "perhaps" and "maybe," for that which you are now doing is now perfect. It is not physical; it is spiritual.

Therefore, no negative ideas shall enter, for negative ideas create a barrier. You shall find that patience is a great rewarder. Humility, humility is a great rewarder. Humbleness of heart opens the door to truth.

All inspiration is of God. That is a golden truth. Man cannot afford to say, "I did it, I am doing it, it is me." It is always God in action.

In God, there is no retrogression. There can be no confusion in God. Man, as you know, is spiritual, individualized in the presence of God. Therefore do not become mortally zealous in that which you are doing, but rather spiritually zealous, and your spiritual zealousness shall never consume you, and there shall never be a question of failure. There may be the appearance of strife, but strife is nonexistent in the presence of God.

Never be fearful of doing good. Let us go to the prophet Job. Remember when he said, "That which I have feared, has come upon me." Never be fearful. When man has an inspiration to do some good, let him use it. Now, we come to the spiritual import of the statement of the Galilean when he said, "Unto he who hath, it shall be added unto, but unto he who hath not, it shall be taken away therefrom, even that which he hath." Now, this sounds like a rather unjust statement, does it not? What is the importance of this statement?

116

The more you use of your talents, love, and inspiration, the more you shall acquire. The less you use of that which you have, the sooner it stagnates and crumbles into the native nothingness. Use your inspiration, let your heart sing and your countenance radiate with a smile, with the joy of the song in your heart. Never become injured in your emotional reaction to what seems an unkindness on the part of others. Man only becomes injured in the manner in which he accepts injury. In the non-acceptance, it is returned to the one who is bent on injuring you through his speaking.

Man only becomes a part of that which he beholds (that which he takes hold of — accepts as a conviction), nothing else. Never look upon injury, never, never. The cruelty or injustice or the misunderstanding, whatever it may be, is a lesson to be learned on the part of the one who created the cruelty, the injury, the misunderstanding. And it is no part of you unless you accept it. Thus, you become a part of the bargain, and then you must appropriate its reaction.

There have been times when each one of you momentarily deviated from the trodden path of spiritual realization; but that was only because the physical or material necessity so made its demand. However, you have quickly returned in humility, and inwardly avowed yourselves to the only true God you know, the God of love. Thus, you have made that which is known to man of Earth a redemption.

117

How well you have served man of Earth shall be revealed to you when you are able to read the emblazoned scroll, written in love, established by yourself to your credit. You will remember there was a man called Peter, and when, "he saw through a glass darkly" as the apostle Paul referred to it in a moment of anxiety, he denied the Presence. Then, "seeing face to face," standing in the reality of spiritual truth, he went forth, no longer a denier but a valiant soldier of the Christ principle of God.

You no longer doubt that which is revealed to you as truth; because of the mental and physical infirmity of those who come to your attention, you are well aware that the power of God is the great physician and that through the renewing of the mind, man can experience the fullness of spirit.

The name, Peter, coming down from the Aramaic, through Hebrew and Greek, the word was and is "petros," meaning light, and what greater blessing can man of Earth become to his fellowman, than he who lights the darkened places? And who abides in greater darkness, than he who abides or dwells in mental darkness, the darkness of superstition, ignorance and fear?

It was upon this "Peter or Petros", that the Christ of God, incarnate in the flesh embodiment, of he who was accepted and known as Jesus, founded the assembly of truth. That is the only church which the Nazarene established; not a building of stone and wood and brick, not made with hands, but that which is eternal in the heavens.

You, dear ones, understand well, and you shall remember that He likewise said, "The kingdom of God is within you." God is always in his heaven and where the kingdom of God is, so is heaven. Heaven then becomes a state of consciousness. Never forget this truth.

You will remember when the Christ incarnate in Jesus appeared before Peter upon the troubled waters, he said to Peter, "It is I." And as long as Peter kept his sight steadfast upon the Christ light, he walked upon the troubled waters. But when he removed his vision from the Christ light, he began to sink and cried unto the Christ light for help. Yes, he cried; he called for help; and because he cried and called, he received.

The Christ light of God inspired the man of Galilee to make this statement, "Seek and you shall find, knock and the door shall be opened, ask, and ye shall receive." What has man to give to his fellowman? The truth! All else fails. And blessed is he or she who walks in the light of spiritual truth and can say to their fellowman, "You are a spiritual being, the image and the likeness of God."

What greater comfort, what greater consolation, what greater succor can man share with his fellowman than sharing the realization that in God, there is no separation? Where there is light, there is no darkness. Where there is truth, there can be no error.

Blessed is he who believes and has neither seen nor heard. God is unseen, God is impersonal, but his wonders can be seen. God becomes personalized through the radiance of the man or woman who, at long last, has risen in consciousness and claimed without fault or failing his oneness with God.

We impose no task; the yoke is easy and the burden is light. Willingness in the service of God and the Council of the ancient mystical White Brotherhood always opens a channel for inspiration. Never be fearful. No one of you ever need be fearful to speak the truth.

It is not always possible to speak the truth, as many of your doctors of Earth, who give sugar-coated pills, have found out. Truth may sound harsh to many who listen, and it may taste a little bitter while it is being swallowed, but it shall ring a bell of happiness. As bitter as the taste may be when the individual is swallowing it, through the process of mental digestion, it shall become sweet as honey. Of course, not one of you are ever going to be rude, ever. That is not necessary, and neither shall you meet with defeat. The further along the path you travel, the greater degree of sensitiveness shall you experience.

When man opens the inner recesses of his spiritual consciousness, he shall understand all that which he perceives through his five physical senses to the degree that he shall be able to separate the wheat from the chaff. Ere long, the power of truth shall have so grown that the man shall no longer desire that which is contrary to truth.

Solomon was expediently wise when he stated, "Get wisdom, get understanding, and forget it not; wisdom is the principle thing." The Galilean said, "I and the Father are one; there are none perfect, no not one. Yea, not even I, but the Father which dwelleth within me." Here Jesus was separating the wheat from the chaff. Do not overlook that fact that, as a young child, He was tutored by the priests of the Levitical temple, but in soul growth, He far surpassed them in understanding. Those who sought to teach Him, when He questioned them, the priests of the temple became frightened.

As He grew into manhood, He walked the highways and the byways of life, holding the torch of truth aloft. He asked none to follow Him, but He held the torch of that divine understanding, incarnate in the flesh habiliment of those who desired to learn; then they, of their own desire, followed Him. His wisdom had become understanding, and thus the understanding shown forth as the divine intelligence of Jesus of Nazareth, the incarnate Christ of God.

Remember, there is but one light, the Christ light, the I AM of God. There is none other and though mortally, man may reject that light, the indwelling Christ (of which man is) cries aloud, "I would behold the light; I would behold the light."

Mark you well, the time shall come when through the region of the solar plexus, in the soul's seat of the sun, though you stand there with your eyes shut tight, you shall feel those who are accepting and those who are rejecting. Remember, nothing is ever permanently rejected, for that which is listened to, establishes a picture. That which is looked upon establishes a picture. Therefore, it is wise for man to listen to the best and to look upon the beautiful.

The only thing man possesses is that which he freely gives, and it costs nothing of earthly fare to give love. The more love is given, the more there is for accumulated love. When man has given up the old understanding for the new understanding, he shall then be in agreement, for, "Behold, the old things have passed away and all things have become new", again. "When I was a child, I spake as a child, but when I became a man, I put away childish things. Then, I did see through a glass darkly, now I see face to face. Faith, hope, love, these three, but the greatest of these is love."

Oh yes, you will find that when man first begins to grow in the light of the Christ, and it becomes necessary for him to meet problems because fellow wayfarers along the path do not understand and are rebellious to the truth, it then may become a trifle difficult to radiate love. Then let it radiate silently, and you shall become the beaconlight upon a rugged coast.

As man wills to decrease his mortal will, it is then he says, "Thy will be done, O Lord." He is saying, "Increase thy image, the light of Divine Intelligence, the Christ mind, increase thy image in wisdom, in me." That is experiencing the regeneration; that is the sum total of humility. "Thy will be done. All there is in the great pattern of life has been, is now, and ever shall be." Humility, humbleness of heart spells success.

Man is a spiritual being; all that the Father is, man becomes in his understanding. He is that now, but he experiences the fullness of the vastness because of his understanding of God.

All that which maintains a perfect balance in life must have a center. The scales of life never balance by but one side. As you are becoming interested in what man has called the secrets of life, you will find, in truth, life holds no secrets. It is only as man does not apply himself. Silence, silence, and in the silence of the soul, desire to become conscious of the oneness of being. Then further desire to become in greater consciousness, the fullness of being. Then with a further desire to understand, all that which rests in the heart center of the Eternal Being. Then as Solomon said, "Speak to the heart of Eternal Being and say, "Give me naught but wisdom, Eternal One, that I may understand."

There is no such thing as sacrifice. There is no such thing as suffering. Man has misinterpreted the

123

words "sacrifice" and "suffering:" they spell but tolerance to circumstances and conditions in what you call life's pattern, faithfulness to principle, but they know no deprivation. Man of Earth cannot deprive himself through faithfulness. When the hour of achievement comes, you will rejoice, and you shall become drunk, but with spiritual wine, which shall not make you drunken.

"Time is not, distance cannot be, memory holds its cherished reflection." All your journeys, all of your progress started with unfaltering faith, faith in others as well as yourself. Faith is necessary in every man, woman, every person that you attract to yourself. Bide your time in faith, each step taken in faith is never lost. The man or woman who goes forth on life's sea with God as the captain, God as a partner, although the path be across seas uncharted and whatever may be his business, having God as a partner in everything that man espouses, that man or woman will never fail.

Woe betide unto the man or woman who says, "I shall lift myself up by my own bootstraps." He will still find himself or she will find herself in the muck and mire of self-righteousness. We reject no man; we draw no line of separation. It matters not to us who man has been; it matters not to us what man is, and we are looking far beyond the contour of the flesh tenement and are beholding the Godman, perfect in the presence of God.

As we have previously said, that looking beyond to the spiritual straightens every crooked road. The crooked body, so to speak, is a crooked road, through which the soul has traveled, but now must make straight the way. That is common sense logic, is it not?

In the world of commerce, there are men and women who are receptive to spiritual leading, but they attribute it to a wisdom of their own. Deception does not last forever, you know. Justice must reign and peace among men in the commercial world must be established.

Liberation of the masses from ignorance must come. Man must learn that he is one in spirit, one in truth, for truth is nonexistent without love. We, of the Council, of the ancient mystical White Brotherhood love you all, and when man of Earth can do likewise, he shall have enriched the universe.

Go forth without fear, continue the service you have rendered, walk in the path of humility, and you shall meet the high price of the calling of God, which is victory over the carnal mind, and the establishment of the Christ mind. This victory will come to you. Those who come to you seeking and all those who cross your path, will touch the aura of your garment, your consciousness, the righteous use of the consciousness of the Christ mind.

Remember, we love you and are every ready to lead you upward to greater illumination.

CHAPTER NINE

GRATITUDE AND RETRIBUTION

Another one of the Brotherhood speaks:

In the ever living presence of God,
There is no death.
Memory holds its cherished reflections,
Love is eternal destiny.
Ah love, which never perishes,
Life which has no end,
God, the ever-living presence,
His love does every broken heart mend,
His light makes bright the places dark
Where man is prone in doubt to wander,
His rod, his staff, they comfort give;
His love, the healing waters.

We heard your call and came to share your love, and in accepting your love, will you accept ours? We are happy to consider this another opportunity to reveal and part the veil of the temple of God, that the light may shine. Truly, he who is seeking and he who understands wends his way to the portals of our sanctum. This is no mystery, for in the light of God's eternal truth, there is no mystery.

All that which you have experienced is but the beginning. The end thereof you seek not. He who walks the path of God beholds not the end of the road. He is but interested in the road and the experiences he will encounter, as he travels the road. There is no weariness of the flesh to him who serves God, as only in his consciousness he would behold weariness.

There are teachers on our side of life, who would be sent and wend their way to you. Man cannot seek to find truth and be unattended. Truly, it has been spoken that the teacher shall be provided in due season. There is no retrogression, it is ever onward, forward and upward. There is no turning back.

You will ever be mindful of this, dear hearts, that he or she on the physical plane, who has dedicated his life to the service of his fellowman, serves God. He or she who goes forth to teach, leads man of Earth from the wilderness of doubt into the light of understanding. With each lesson the teacher expounds, he or she, too, grows, even as the student. Growth is eternal. As your heart's desire sends forth the clarion call for guidance, thus attracting to you various teachers, you are rendering unto God a most precious service.

Why should there be a teacher, if there is no one to be taught? Therefore we admonish you to continue your quest. Whatever seeming disappointments you may have experienced in that which you have learned to call the past (disappointments because of the seeming expressions of ingratitude), were but at the time when you were passing through the regeneration. You will remember, in previous discourses, we have mentioned that the paths of men do not cross, one touching the other, but for the reason that they have crossed before.

When has man given and when has man received? Volumes upon volumes have been written upon the law of retribution. Read as you may, truth is but revealed through experience, and in no other manner. It is a blessing that all of the past is not revealed to man, lest he would live in greater self-accusation than he does.

It is but mortal to question why there is seeming disappointment. Have we not mentioned, dear ones of God, that each experience is a lesson? Have we not likewise mentioned, when appearance of adversity makes itself known, or shall we say, when retribution makes itself known through the appearance of adversity, let man say to himself, "How have I earned this? I shall meet the challenge of life with love."

You will remember we have likewise spoken to you in this manner, whenever it becomes man's opportunity to render a kindness, it is but because somewhere along life's path, and the path is endless, there has been a kindness rendered. Now that you have met the challenge, and it has become your desire to follow the path of regeneration, you will find that you will no longer be deceived, as deception is understood.

Each one whom you meet shall carry a scale and upon that scale, in its balance, they shall weigh their own worthiness or unworthiness. We have told you that now, in this present incarnation, you have met with those who expressed ungratefulness. We do not deny having agreed with you that it was a lesson to you also; therefore do not measure yourself short with the yardstick of judgment. Judge no one. You were worthy, and you remain worthy, and the appearance of unworthiness expressed upon the part of those unto whom you bestowed your kindness can never destroy your worthiness.

You will find that lesson beautifully narrated in the 6th and 7th chapters of the book according to the record of St. Matthew. "Let the dead bury the dead." Those who express ingratitude injure but themselves. It cannot come nigh your dwelling, only as you accept it, and you shall never accept ingratitude. It is not yours. Remember, you did not create it; your graciousness did not express it.

Shall you say to yourself (and I am speaking of that part of life's path previous to this embodiment), "Where along the path could I have expressed ingratitude? It must have been, or it would not be so expressed to me." Remember, dear ones, do not accept ingratitude as an injury. Listen: do not accept it as an injury, for it has not injured; you have met the challenge and the record is cleared and clean. The ingratitude expressed has not depleted your resources. Stop for a moment and reason to the contrary. Dear ones, your increase has been multiplied.

Ingratitude cannot impoverish those who express through love. That is not in keeping with the law of God.

All that man enjoys, even though he has experienced ingratitude, is proof sufficient that the love he expressed has blessed both himself and the one upon whom it was bestowed.

Let's go back again to ingratitude. Cut loose, send back that which does not belong to you, since you did not create it. Send it back with a blessing of love, even as you expressed yourself in love in the beginning. For the Master has said, "I shall not look for sacrifice, I shall have mercy." For every comfort and peace of mind you are enjoying at this very hour, it is because some kindness expressed in love dropped from the extended hand, your hand. Remember, "Let the dead bury their own dead."

131

Look not over your shoulder at that which man calls the past, not even a peek. Moreover, say to yourself, "My ship of state is on the high seas. It rides in peaceful waters and knows no storm." If man could look into the record book in the heart's consciousness of those who express ingratitude, man would say, "Thank God, I behold not such in the record of my heart."

You shall not labor in vain. The yoke shall be easy and the burden light. In truth, you shall not want. In truth, you shall be able to say, "The Lord (law) is my shepherd, I shall not want (all my needs are supplied). My Father, our Father, who art in heaven, hallowed, loving, adorable, revered in my heart is Thy name." Love is the precious ointment. It is the balm of Gilead. Love always expresses a happy appreciation when it sees love being expressed through another's hand, for love is the ointment from the alabaster box of devotion. Love heals. Live, dear hearts, and help others to live through the love that God pours forth, using you as the vehicle of his oil of love.

CHAPTER TEN

SPIRITUAL RICHES

One of the Brotherhood speaks:

To each one of you we bestow a blessing, and we are grateful for your continued spiritual quest. Man cannot defeat the Law of God, and as man will use the Law of God righteously, God shall continue to supply all of man's needs. Therefore may I refer to the lonely, humble Galilean when he said, "According to the riches of God, according to the riches in the glory of God, shall your needs be supplied."

At this very moment, nature, Mother Nature, is producing and reproducing, producing and reproducing, which is proof positive, that the world is never coming to an end. There may be an end of cycles; the culmination of periods of time, but the world shall never come to an end, for God is endless.

There is nothing before God, there is nothing without God, God is all there is, the sum total of all life. Blessed is the man who followeth not in the seat of the ungodly, nor sitteth in the seat of the scornful, for his delight is the Law of God. He shall be as a tree, planted by the rivers of the waters of life, and his leaf shall not wither.

Unto each man of Earth, after his own desire, comes forth that which man has learned to call experience. There was a time when we, too, trod the physical plane of life. Some of our number experienced rebirth upon rebirth. Now those of us who have been here through what you of Earth call ages, single out those who now travel the mundane plane, that their time shall be so employed that upon release from the physical body, they shall find here, within our number, their priestly inheritance.

It is possible for members of our Council to work out to the minutest detail all that is necessary for man (physically incarnate) to know. But it would mean depriving man of the necessary growth. Therefore we are desirous of planting tiny seeds, sufficiently large enough, small as they may be, that man may nurture them with his every precious goodly desire. In so doing, see the seeds grow forth, expressing every possible beauty. It is well for man to think and his think-ing should at all times be constructive.

There are many on the mundane sphere of life who say, "Why the necessity of prayer?" Prayer is but another form of expressing thoughts. Prayer is a pro-found manner of thinking, particularly so when man's prayer is a prayer of thanksgiving. While in a state of prayerful meditation, man is opening the door whence all wisdom may enter.

As strange and mysterious as it may appear to man, when prayer is not immediately answered, it is because man has failed in his thinking to recognize the goodness, the graciousness of all that which he has experienced.

All prayer is answered, even that which, at times, is not immediately supplied. For that power which man has learned to call God knows the answer to man's desires before they are expressed. Quite often, man prays for the granting of some favor, and that power, known to man as God, says, "My Child, you are not ready for that, when you have grown, you shall have it."

Time passes, and in that which man calls the far distant future, that request is granted, but man fails to recognize the source from which it has come. He fails to recognize, in what he has called the long ago, the prayer for that particular favor. Whether he remembers or not, he shall graciously say, "I thank you, God. For out of the fullness of the heart of Eternal Love, this has come to me."

Remember, all error is but temporary. That is true, but it retards man's growth. Therefore, in speaking to someone, in aiding someone with a problem, speak words of wisdom wisely and carefully. Watch the expression of the faces of those with whom you speak and you shall understand whether they are, or are not accepting.

Put yourself in their position, remembering when you started your quest for spiritual knowledge. When you see their brows wrinkled and their countenance express resentment, you shall know that you have given a sufficient amount for that time. Then let your conversation be in terms in which they are familiar. That is sowing the seed. You will see their countenance change, and inwardly, they are saying, "Now he is selling us something we understand."

As they open their thinking to that which they do understand, the seeds you have dropped fall into fertile soil, and they will be able to accept them. They will be able to accept them with that which they understand. The seeds will find lodgment in a fertile mental womb. In due time, a new babe, a new idea shall be born.

Whatever your religious intentions have been, hold fast. Whatever your conception of God has been, let it now become quickened in truth. How well you dear ones of Earth understand that the Infant (as you refer to the lowly born body of Jesus) must learn. Yet, in consciousness, the soul of the tiny infant body has all understanding necessary, for it has traveled life's sands myriads of times.

But you will say to us of the Council, "Why does it have to learn when it has all the wisdom necessary? May we be privileged to ask you, why was it necessary to return?" For the reason that mortal confusion proved to be a barrier to the expression of Divine Wisdom.

It is never necessary for man to leave his body, to become wise unto the creative power of that which man has recognized as God. Therefore, it is our desire, at this time, to lead you in the first steps of higher understanding in truth. Man is a child of the great cosmic universe. As man grows spiritually, he expresses the Great Oversoul, and he begins to realize that reincarnation is a living truth and a reality.

It is for that reason we desire collaborators and teachers with whom we may entrust lessons, with the message of life. We would not speak in derogatory terms of the many teachers who have endeavored to teach the story of life. When we do find a man or woman who is willing, who will, with the regenerated will, forsake phantoms and fancy as well as fables, to walk in the path of God's light, we call that one. Again, we repeat to those who are answering the call and making the choice: it is they who become the chosen ones of their own individual choice.

137

Learn this truth well and no longer will life be a mystery to you. Listen, dear hearts, there is but one God. Regardless of how the myriad teachers have taught, there is but one God; there is but one life; there is but one manifestation in the absolute of God.

Would you meet the Christ of God, as you walk along the highways and the byways of life? As you behold your fellowman, regardless of the outward appearances of the physical habiliment, you behold and you will meet the Christ of God.

For remember, the physical habiliment cannot express life without the indwelling Christ of God. Creeds, ceremonies, rituals, and mantrums are not of Christ, in the presence of God. Do not deny the Living God because of man-conceived rituals. It is for that reason it became necessary for the birth of the Infant habiliment. Man has become deceived. Behold the light, for the light dispels all darkness. The Galilean came to teach truth.

Man has erected shrines, altars, and temples in dedication to the humble Galilean. The Galilean walked the road; he entered temples which man had erected for only one reason, to tell the story of the Living God. You will remember his words when he said, "And in that day, when ye shall cry unto me, `Lord, Lord, have I not healed the sick? Have I not cast out devils? Have I not thus and so, thus and so, in Thy name?' I shall say unto ye, depart from me ye workers of iniquity, I know thee not."

Now, when man expresses himself as "mixed up in a problem," who is mixing what you refer to as a problem? Be still and be unpersuaded by mortal mind, and you shall get the answers, just as you have in that which you refer to as the past.

Humility, dear hearts! All the assurance of man-made forgiveness is worthless unless man forgives himself. For if man does not forgive, where is there room in man's thinking for the forgiveness, which the prefect or the potentate has assured man of?

Can you fill a vessel with water when it is already filled, without losing some of the water? You have a term for it, you say, "It is wasted." Wasted, wasted, wasted! Keep the chalice of your heart clean and bright, and as it is filled with the wine of life, which is God's love, drink of it, share it with your fellowman, that there may be more room for more wine and never, never any of it wasted.

Our message to you, dear hearts, is this: you are God's children. There is no man-made ceremony which can bring you closer to God than you have been from the beginning, and that statement is truth. Be not deceived. Evil communications corrupt good manners.

It does not pay for any individual to become emotionally disturbed. It is well for man to become concerned about the physical things of life, which are of very little consequence, as far as his physical well-being is concerned, or his peace of mind. We do not mean for man to be negligent, as the word negligence

139

is understood, but there can be much stress and strain placed upon what man calls physical order.

There shall never be any task imposed, only the manner, mortally so, in which you may conceive of a service to be rendered as a task. Always remember, your fellowman has the same right to live his portion of life's pattern as you desire to live yours. The truth may be ever so real to you as proven in life's pattern beyond every shadow of a doubt. Yet, never proselytize.

Long before you ever knew anything about the ancient mystical White Brotherhood, you perhaps knew about it, but it was a hidden mystery. You were receiving your inspiration and guidance. As you have received in the past, so shall you continue to receive inspiration and guidance.

Quiescence is the key. When man is quiet, when he is happy with his neighbor and finding no fault with himself and his neighbor, then he is standing on the threshold of the door to the highest possible state of mental ecstasy. Therein lies every treasure for man to claim.

When you can share light with others, share it. When you can speak a word of truth, speak it. Be every willing and ready to share the story of life.

Humility will carry you well along the path. Whatever may be your rank or station in life, mortally so, never let it become a screen of deception, never. Remember, the physical habiliment, barefoot and covered with tatters and rags, besmeared and besmirched perchance with the grime of the day, that physical habiliment is the dwelling place of the Christ of God.

Now, why are we making these statements? Let us take you back. As you were living life's pattern, you were not constantly in a serious frame of mind; you mixed pleasure with contemplation, with the reverie which brought peace of mind and peace to your body.

There is a time for man to laugh, a time for what he has called play and also for what he has understood as serious time. Man can better relax, meditate, concentrate, and be a trifle serious (if you care to call it such) after he has a bit of recreation. The physical body is justified in having recreation, for then one is relaxed, happily so. Man was never intended to live a drab inharmonious life.

Consequently, you were able to relax, and let us remind you, please, quite frequently when you were not expecting inspiration, it was there. Do you remember? Yes, without seeking for it? Remember: a merry heart maketh for good medicine.

Spiritual riches are ever tangible, never lost, as you understand the word lost. Moths do not corrupt spiritual riches. Neither can rust corrupt, nor thieves break through and steal. He who is spiritually rich is rich, indeed. All else is transitory, constantly going through some experience, changing either to the mountain's heights or the valley's depths.

141

But when man of Earth is spiritually rich, he shall have sufficient light with which to hold fast to that of worldly accumulation which has come from the Father. Remember, man does not dare to possess even the physical habiliment in which he dwells. Therefore the Nazarene said to the rich young ruler, "Give all thou hast and follow me." Also, "Evil communication corrupts good manners." For the rich young ruler had heard them corrupt his good manner, and his first thought was of his earthly possessions, and he forgot his earthly possessions were not his.

What did the Nazarene mean when he said, "Give all thou hast and follow me?" Give himself, for all the rich young ruler possessed was himself. His earthly wealth was but loaned to him for a season because of the goodness and the abundance of God.

God is man's house, and though you are sitting in your home, in a physical habiliment, you know well that you are ever in the presence of God. Now, when man has learned that lesson, he shall have no fear, for even though his fellowman betray him, as you understand the word betrayal, he shall overlook the betrayal and behold the Christ of God, even in he or she whom he calls a betrayer.

Betrayal is a mortal weakness. There shall never anything cross your path, dear hearts, but what it is a lesson, a lesson disregarded in a former incarnation. Man of Earth has never endured an adversity but what he has earned it; do not overlook that fact.

When you claim your spiritual riches, you shall be able to meet any adversity which may thereafter follow. When man comes closer to God, the path becomes bright with the light of God, and the peace of God comes to man's thinking and fewer are the adversities. Man only becomes disappointed because he expects too much. Remember the words of the apostle Paul, when he said, "These three, but the greatest of these is love."

We are looking into that which man of Earth has called the future; therefore in accepting any duties, whatever they may be, there may be moments when your physical assistance is necessary, in addition to your spiritual aid. Humility is ever the watchword. Let it be understood that any duty is never in the way of a command or a demand. We do not desire at any time to deprive any of our dear collaborators of their time necessary to the peace, happiness, and welfare of their own individual manner of living life's pattern.

Accept your part or pattern of service, regardless of what it may be, without feeling or accepting any injustice or injury to yourselves, individually or collectively. Remember, the field is heavy with grain and the garners are few. The vines are heavy-laden with the ripened fruit.

As you labor in love, in peace, and harmony, with humility ever your watchword, you shall place the ripened fruit in the storehouse where it shall benefit humanity. You shall garner the grapes which hang upon the vine and place them in the winepress of life.

143

From them, you shall bring forth the sweet nectar of peace and happiness to your fellowman.

The wheat and the blood of the grape, and that which man of Earth in dedication to his God renders unto his fellowman, brings spiritual riches. All the wealth of the universe is meaningless, without spiritual riches. When the fruit of your labors brings peace and comfort to some troubled hearts, you shall be rich indeed, rich unto the richness of God, as well as the richness unto the marrow of your bones. Remember, unselfish loving service, as unto the Father, ever renews the strength of the body.

Now, remember, that of service you render is to be considered always as "unto God." As you render it in humility and love, you render it unto your fellowman. What is the first requisite of humility? The lowly Galilean understood this when He said, "Of myself, I am nothing. It is the Father which dwelleth within me." This is surrender in dedication, and humbleness of heart.

Now, those of you who have heard the call and answered, you may yet turn your attention in the opposite direction, if you so will, if you feel that our lessons, our admonitions are too difficult to accept. If you yet will follow on with the choice you have made, you will pass through the gate to the illumination of the great white light of the Eternal Cosmos.

Within the innermost depths of your heart's consciousness, you avow yourself, not by word of lip to man of Earth, and not by lip to God. For God hears the unspoken word, and you shall speak it in the silence of your heart's consciousness. Remember, beloved, should you at any time, as you understand time, desire to withdraw, we, of the Council, never forsake you nor disavow you; because at some time along life's path, which is endless, you shall again pick up the threads upon life's loom. You shall finish the pattern.

Woe unto the man or woman who seeks fame and fortune without spiritual riches, for he has become as sounding brass and a tinkling cymbal. He yet sees through a glass darkly and has not yet arisen in consciousness, where he sees face to face with his God. Remember, humility, humility is ever the watchword.

Happier is the way, however, when you walk in the light of truth. We assure you, you can keep your avowal, for you have all assumed greater mortal responsibilities and have kept them very well. Fear not; remember, "His rod and His staff shall comfort you."

There are many who are seeking for health of body and peace of mind. There are those who are knocking upon the door of the storehouse of God's infinite supply. There are those who are asking and those who shall continue to speak, to knock, and to ask. This is the reason we seek and search for collaborators, for teachers, through whom we can open the way, that they shall not need to seek long; they shall not need to knock in desperation and anxiety. They shall not have to ask in a pleading, beggardly manner, for God has already provided. You shall not labor in vain, for you are not accepting your labor as a task, but more as a duty; not as an imposed task, for you have graciously accepted through patience, for devotion is patience. Patience always reveals sincerity of devotions.

We bless you in your path of service. Mind you well, the path of life which you have trod has not been strewn with roses and each one of you has sipped from an unsweetened cup. It is only he, who has felt the pangs, who can feel the pangs suffered by his fellow-man. It is only he, who has sipped from the empty cup, who knows of the emptiness thereof. Listen and remember the words of the Galilean when, after he had been scourged, spat upon, vilified, persecuted and offered the bitter cup, said, "Father, forgive them, for they know now what they do." The oil of God's love now anoints you and the tapers of righteous illumination burn in your heart's consciousness, as you have ignited it. Let your light shine. We bless each one of you; rejoice and be exceedingly glad, for great is your reward in heaven.

And the Galilean said, "Know ye not that the kingdom of God is within you?"

With this assurance, God is not afar off. Silent prayer is the manner in which you talk with your God, and in silence, you hear the answer. Never in commotion, confusion, never; silence ever. Silence is the avenue that leads to God. Silence removes chaos and confusion. You hold the key which turns the lock in the door to the storehouse of God's infinite riches. Use it! Bless you ever, world without end.

Our parting word to you from our Elder Brother, Elder Teacher: "I have come unto my own, and ye have received me. Bless you a thousand times ten thousand. Bless you, bless you, bless you."

CHAPTER ELEVEN

WALKING THE STREET CALLED STRAIGHT

A member of the Brotherhood speaks:

> Come, walk the street called Straight,
> Give me the mold, give me the die,
> I shall destroy it for you, my child.
> Love, your comforter shall be
> Look not back upon the misery
> The mold did hold, the die did cast,
> That now is in the past.
> Follow me on the street called Straight.
> The time is yet, it is not late,
> I Am God, Father, Friend.
> Unto thee I grant

Unto that which man has called the end
We walk the street called Straight.
Crooked roads have ends to meet
But straightened roads, no end doth greet.
— Tis on and on to the great white light
You see, my child, as you walk
The street called Straight.

We are happy to greet you, beloved, for there is an open door to the Father's house. You now stand before that open door, hands outstretched. You now see beyond that open door. There are anxious faces, tear-stained eyes. Weary, worn bodies wait. They wait for you, dear ones, to lead them through the open door.

Restless become the thoughts of he or she who, in his soul's consciousness, does say, "Father, you have called; I have chosen to follow," and then leave the street called Straight. As man is called and the man chooses to follow, he is not asked to sign a scroll nor speak his vow. He but ascribes himself to his God, as he beholds his God on the street called Straight.

Man is not bound, he is forever free. With the same freedom that God gives man, let man never attempt to deny his fellowman equal freedom.

Beloved, there is an altar. It is within your heart's consciousness, and upon that altar rests the priceless treasure. It is as a newborn infant; it shall grow and he who does not have the patience to endure with the growth of the infant, let him, with honor in his heart say, "Father, I desire to release myself."

God holds no man in bondage. And when the man who tastes of the bitter cup in that which he calls the bitter past and empties it to the final dregs, only to have it filled with the blood of the sweet grape, becomes impatient, then let him pass his cup to another who is willing to drink of it. God does not bind; there is no bondage in God.

God's will is free, and to understand the freedom of God's will, man makes no imperfect mold and casts no imperfect die. God's will is the die which cuts the true pattern. God's will is the mold in which man molds his perfect portion of life. Let no man of Earth measure his future by the measuring rod of discrepancy, of that which is known as the past.

Impatience is the measuring rod of discrepancy. Impatience has caused every evil which has ever befallen man. Is it too difficult for man to be tolerant with truth? Is it too difficult for man to walk the street called Straight? What shall man do?

Let man say, "What have I to do with this?" Man meets nothing along life's path but what he has created. That which man beholds through the five physical senses, man becomes a part of. Therefore we have in our previous visits admonished against covetousness. You are about to experience a great revelation, but it shall not serve its purpose unless it is looked upon with love.

151

We shall not deceive you, you are precious in the presence of God. Each child is worthy of all that which he possesses. Let no man of Earth say it is God's desire that man should deprive and deny himself to serve God.

Serving God brings abundance into full fruition. Man finds it as he walks the street called Straight. It is God's will, the perfect will, that man's heart's desire be plentifully, abundantly filled.

The God of truth is not cruel; does not rule with a rod of wrath; does not deceive. Remember, evil communications corrupt good manners. The teachers of Earth who teach a God of cruelty should be mindful, lest the God of whom they teach measures unto them the manner in which they teach.

Let man think before he speaks. Hasty thinking, hasty speech, hasty action! Uncomfortable conditions arise and that is the manner in which man makes the mold and casts the die. How frequently do we hear, "If I had only known differently."

Beloved, now you know, now you see. Temper your wisdom with understanding. Lift your physical bodies in health, strength, peace and power. Live with your God in His heaven, there lies the street called Straight.

There is an old hymn man used to sing: "Take time to be holy, speak oft with thy Lord." How is man to do this? It is not difficult, it perhaps is so simple that it is overlooked.

Breathe a part of your life into your fellowman, so to speak. Remember, dear hearts, there is but one Presence in the universe. For that which man has used as a weapon of destruction shall be converted into a mantle of protection. Thus shall come to pass the statement as it was written, "Man shall beat the swords into plowshares and till the soil, for in that day, the sword of wrath shall be sheathed forever." For there is a God on the street called Straight.

In the Holy Writ, you will read of the Master Jesus, called the Christ. He said, "I must withdraw, but I shall leave with you a Comforter." That Comforter is but the enlarging of one's own individual self, the spiritual self.

That is the Comforter man shall share, where sharing is a necessity, spiritually so. For the greatest sharing is spiritual. When man shares spiritually, all needs are supplied. When needs are supplied, wants never become known.

Let man become wise unto God's wisdom. There is an old hymn that man used to sing and some still do: "There are no disappointments in heaven." Now, where is heaven? It is within man's consciousness. When man becomes spiritually awakened, spiritually satisfied, there are then no disappointments.

> When peace, like a river, attendeth my way,
> When sorrow, like sea billows roll,
> Whatever my lot, thou has taught me to say,
> It is well, it is well, with my soul.

153

When man understands that soul and spirit are one, and being one, are indestructible, the infirmities of the flesh vanish. God speaks spiritually.

In the beginning was the Word and the Word became flesh. And the Word continued to become flesh. Woe to man of Earth who says to another, "It cannot be done, you cannot do it. You will never heal your body." That is a word, is it not? Should man be prone to accept that word? Whether he speaks it audibly or not, he is using that word, is he not? He is creating the flesh within his temple, either that of dis-ease, if it be contrary to truth, or wholeness of the body, if it is in harmony with truth.

God is the perfect word. Hence, the truth of the Nazarene, "Man liveth not by bread alone, but by every word which proceedeth from the mouth of God." God speaks truth. God is positive. Now is the accepted time. There is no tomorrow. Tomorrow becomes today. Yesterday was but another day. All the good is to be remembered. Whatever has been contrary to good is to be forgotten, if it was ever recognized. Now is the accepted time.

Remember, each one of you, this is the working of the Law of God. Listen carefully, should anyone be in need of assistance, ask them, "What do you desire more than anything else in the world?" You who feel the weight of their chaos, their desire should be peace of mind, health of body, these two. With peace of mind and health of body, all needs are satisfied.

154

Health of body is the child of peace of mind. Having peace in God, for having peace of mind in God is having peace with God. When man's thinking is at peace, he reaches forth into the fullness of the Eternal Cosmos, which man has learned to call God.

Mind you well, dear hearts, there is only one mind: the mind of God, and so as man rises in consciousness, free from all that which is sordid and troublesome, he touches the mind of God. The greatest desire in the world, the greatest treasure, is peace of mind.

Listen, each one of your fellowman is entitled, by right of birth, according to his choice, his desire to follow that path of his choice. Man, mortally, is to be helped. Regardless of the path he pursues religiously, grant it to him, grant it to him. Be he of the Roman faith, the Anglican faith, etc., it matters not, as long as expressing faith in what he believes will aid him to find his God.

But do not proselytize. Every man has a right to believe in that which he desires to believe. There is only one desire that you should have, and that is helping man to understand that God is a living reality. Also, that he shall ever bow mentally in humble genuflection before God. It is, therefore for that reason we have likewise said, "No negative thinking." God is my fortress; God is my shield and buckler; God is my all of everything, that is, I am God's child."

O yes, there may be the appearance as man understands it, with a twinge of pain or some other manner

155

of physical defect. You know, dear hearts, the bell of the belfry of a church rings forth calling man to worship. Go and commune with the Father.

The sages of the Far East sound their cymbals, calling their own to worship. So what is pain in the physical body; how is man to understand it? It is the bell in the church belfry ringing forth, "Come let us worship; I am not afraid; I live, I live, I live, thank God, I thank you, Father." Rest and claim it: your strength and oneness with the Father; claim it, for there is much work to do.

You are gleaners, harvesters in the field. Claim your birthright, live in the fullness of God's light and love; let nothing discourage you, for you are co-rulers with God now.

CHAPTER TWELVE

DEDICATED TO THE PRESENCE OF GOD

One of the Brotherhood speaks:

> There is but one Presence, the Pres-
> ence of God the good.
> There is but one Presence in the
> universe, God the good.
> I am now immersed in Perfect Being,
> God the good.
> The created Presence of God in all
> mankind of Earth,
> I behold God the Good.
> May I ever see in spirit and in truth
> The Perfect Being! God the good.

And thus in Earth, in Perfect Being
All life, which I behold immersed in
   God the good,
May my inner eye be single ever unto
   the light;
The light of Perfect Being, God the
   good.

For eons of time, the masters of the ancient mystical White Brotherhood have waited for the opportunity of sharing with you the light of truth. As the Nazarene has spoken, so it has become evident in your life when he said, "I have come that they might have life and have it more abundantly." Also, from the pen of a poet has fallen the following:

Would you have life abundant?
   Love doubles for All you give;
There is a means no surer than
   helping someone to live.

In this very hour, when many are interested in destruction, your lives have been dedicated to life and life more abundantly. As you lay your head on its pillow of rest, lay it there, dear ones, with the assurance that your waking moments have not been wasted, nor lived in vain.

There are many dear souls who have a desire to reincarnate and return to the Earth plane as teachers.

Thus the vacancies they leave shall be filled by the souls that have served on the inner plane, who are on our side of life waiting, having been instructed, and ready to move forward.

There are no plans to be made for immediate procedure, for remember, plans are not necessary when desire is righteous. As we have previously discussed, plans quite often savor with the misguidance of the unregenerated centers. You have acquired knowledge, and the knowledge which you have acquired has led you into the path of wisdom. Now, the Godman, of which you are a part, is beginning to enfold you in the fullness of divine principle.

Man never knows the length and breadth or the depth of the words he utters, but it eventually comes to pass and at an unexpected moment, you hear the great tidings of good news. As you have walked along the path of life, you have lifted many who have been burdened.

The joy of living is the joy of giving. When the word "giving" is mentioned, the average individual thinks of sharing something physical or material, and that is well. However, the greatest giving and the greatest sharing is more often in the speaking of a kindly word, a silent prayer. Such is never lost and the seemingly intangible becomes the tangible; that which is spiritual never perishes.

Remember the words of the lowly Galilean, "Our yoke is easy, our burden light." You will never hear from any member of the Council these words, "You must, it is our command, it is our demand." You will never hear that. For according to the richness of your desire is the glory or the beneficence which you experience. You shall always be willing and ready in full surrender and love to tell the story of that which sustains you, prospers you, and keeps your every affair in perfect order.

For those of you who are so desirous to dedicate yourselves, we shall be waiting to lead you through the gate of illumined consciousness to the full awareness of your divinity and that of all mankind. Continue to follow the light of life as it is now.

There shall be a day, however, in the advancement of mortal man, when guidance from the world that man now calls the unknown, shall be accepted in its truth and entirety. Man uses the term, "History repeats itself," and in that experience of mortal man which man of Earth refers to as the Dark Ages of the past, mortal man then relied upon that which was gathered from the so-called "world of the unknown." As man advances, he again shall come to the realization that there is nothing hidden.

There is an Eternal Source of Wisdom, and it is from the Eternal Source of Wisdom (call it what you will) that all revealings come forth. It is for that reason that disembodied man finds mortal man in a receptive or what is known as a passive state. That is brought about in man's thinking, mortal man's thinking, in order that the contact be properly established.

There is no wisdom other than Eternal Wisdom, there cannot be, for man is an eternal being. When mortal man makes a careful analysis of the wisdom of the masters, man will find the wisdom has its origin in one eternal womb. Call it God, Nature, call it what you will. Let man of Earth not be interested in labels or titles or any particular categories. Let man become interested in the Eternal Source and then man shall not be misguided.

We of the Council can explain it briefly in this manner. There is but one mind, what man has learned to call the mind of God. Mortal man must make contact with that Eternal Mind. How does man accomplish that contact? Through but one known avenue known as thought.

It is therefore a statement of truth that, "as man thinketh in his heart, so is he." As we have mentioned before, the heart of man is found in the uppermost part of the human form known as the head or cranium, commonly referred to as the brain. Now, God, or Principle, resides in the brain only as man thinks in terms of God mind or Godlike. Regardless to what degree man is in contradiction with that statement, it does not make it of less value in truth.

When man thinks Godward or Godlike, he is claiming the power of that which is known as superconscious mind. In his constructive thinking, he has tapped the eternal source of supply. Hence, rebirth is truth. As mortal man uses the term, "eventually," eventually, man shall be one with the Infinite.

To those dear ones who are continuing their pursuit in spiritual light here and now, in this incarnation, this pursuit annihilates all desire to return again to claim another physical habiliment, to finish the lesson; you can finish it now.

The greatest barriers to the great illumination are criticism, doubt, intolerance, and self-gratification. The last is the greatest of those barriers. Therefore we continually suggest humility. Again we say, call it what you will: God, Nature, Supreme Principle, it is not the name, the title, the category in which it is placed. It is the recognition and then the application.

Whatever is acquired in man's sojourn along the physical highway of life, the recognition of these, be they material wealth or talents, it shall be done in wise, "Through whatever avenue I have acquired these, whether it be by the sweat of my brow or by my leisure, I have acquired it because of the abundance of the oneness with the Eternal Principle of life."

If we, of the Council, were to mention our regard, our respect, our love, our admiration for the various physical channels we are permitted to express through, we could express it, not in many words, but with one word, humility. It is the humble soul that becomes the receptive channel, the soul that is not carried away by self-gratification. Humility is the key of the receptive soul and sincere prayer of gratitude is the first approach to humility. "It is not I who doeth the work, but the Father, the Divine Presence, who dwelleth within." "I and the Father are one." The Divine Presence: "All I am is of the great I AM," one with the Father, the eternal, Divine Principle within.

Always remember the principle known to man of Earth as Father, is Father and Mother. Therefore man of Earth shall learn to say, "Father-Mother God" and "All I am, all I possess is of the Father."

How many men and women of your mortal plane had the rude awakening to find themselves (as it is so explained in the mortal plane) penniless, because they had been used to fabulous sums and never gave recognition to the Presence as the source through which the fabulous sums did come? They were unable to meet the mortal crises and resorted to that which man of Earth knows as "taking their own life."

When mortal power, mortal prestige, mortal rank, mortal station were removed, all were only tangible, and the spiritual had been neglected, there was nothing for man to cling to. Therefore when the humble Nazarene was breaking his farewell crust of bread, he said, "Before the cock crows twice, I shall be denied, I shall be betrayed, I shall be forsaken."

Each of the chosen twelve said, "Is it I, Lord, is it I?" Peter said, "Master, I shall die with thee." But Peter thrice denied before the cock crowed, Judas betrayed, Thomas doubted, and the man Jesus stood physically alone before Caiphas, his accuser. From the outer court, Peter listened, ashamed and afraid to be known as a disciple of the humble Nazarene.

Judas betrayed Jesus, and in so betraying, betrayed his own birthright with the Presence, for thirty pieces of silver. Yet they had lifted the cup together, they had broken bread together, a physical act in which they had pledged their spiritual allegiance, but they beheld it not in consciousness.

When the spiritual presence that once tenanted the physical habiliment of the man Jesus, when that spiritual presence entered a room through doors that were locked and barred, there were but eleven disciples left, and they cringed in terror. Judas had destroyed his physical habiliment. How does man of Earth lock himself away from the Presence? How? Through the act of self-righteousness, not spiritual righteousness, which is a dedication unto the Presence.

Again, may we repeat, God is no respecter of persons, and God can only become personified through the manner in which mortal man, in his thinking, desires to rise into the height of Godmind and personify the Godmind in his portion of life's pattern as it is allotted to him to live. It is as simple as that.

That is the message we are desirous of passing to man through the physical collaborators whom we call and who choose to follow. Man can only be as Godlike as he, in his thinking, desires to be, and desire creates

164

the pattern. Man lives the pattern as he created it in his desire, be it one incarnation or many. For in Divine Principle, a day is likened unto a thousand years and a thousand years unto a day.

Though there may be persecutions and rejections of truth and of those who reveal it, there shall ever remain the chosen. What do we mean by chosen ones of God? God has chosen all his creation, but when man decides to choose truth from error, right from wrong, he has chosen the path of good or God; for it is his conscious awareness of the truth of being that makes the choice.

Man's consciousness illumined from the torch of truth is well worth whatever manner of persecution you may endure. Man is led step by step because he questions his ability to understand. Questioning one's ability to understand proves to be a smoke screen, as it were, before the altar of revealing.

Man accomplishes nothing, mortally, that is worthwhile. All that is accomplished is done so from the power of God. When man shall live at peace with himself and live at peace with his fellowman, there shall no longer be destructive criticism in his thought structure. He then shall ascend through the regeneration, beyond the confines (the narrow confines, if you please) of the mortal.

When educators of schools and universities shall cease to denounce God, they shall accept God. When that day dawns, they shall discover that all education they know anything about came from the one source and the center of life: God.

Can man create a blade of grass? Can man create a rose? Can man create in his test tube, or otherwise, the glory of a physical habiliment? When he can create that through mortal achievement, which he shall never be able to do, man can sustain life but man cannot create life, so let man search his knowledge, spiritually.

God is not a form. God is not a creed. God is truth. There is but one light in the universe, the Christ light of God. Man may climb over the wall into the sheepfold, but he could not enjoy the peace and comfort of the sheepfold because he did not have the experience of passing through the door.

Man lives in the physical habiliment because he so chooses to do. His choice to so live in the physical habiliment is but to have the physical experience of passing through the door of the sheepfold. In so doing, he is undoing the mistakes of the past.

Life is eternal, and well that it is. For when man becomes obstinate with himself in his thinking, it would be merciless if he had not other incarnations in which to overcome himself and his unmerciful acts with himself and his fellowman. There are many people who are groping in darkness, darkness of their own will and desire, because they know no other way. Perhaps you may say to me, "Can all mankind be reached?"

When man or woman becomes sufficiently interested in his fellowman or the spiritual entity and forgets about outward appearances or mannerisms, and beholds his fellowman as a spiritual entity as God created it, then all mankind can be reached.

Woe unto the one who feasts upon his own knowing and with his idle hands folded upon his bosom says, "I am secure; let the other fellow find his own way." Woe betide him, for as we have repeatedly stated, the harvest is great, but the gleaners are few.

Man of Earth has created denominations, not God. Man of Earth has created groups, socially, which is another barrier. Social aspiration may be all right in its place, but when it causes man to deny his fellowman, then it is no longer of God.

Tyranny has accomplished nothing in any individual's life. Therefore let no man of Earth, nor any woman of Earth, ever become tyrannical with themselves in their thinking. It is sufficient to be able to overcome one's own individual mistakes, but it is with greater difficulty that man overcomes the mistakes of his fellowman, which he, himself, perchance is the cause of his fellowman making. Think this through well.

You are familiar with the prayer, a part of which is in this wise, "Give us this day our daily bread," meaning spiritual sustenance. You have correlative passages of Scripture, "Man liveth not by bread alone, but by every word which proceedeth forth from the mouth of God."

When the daily bread becomes established in consciousness, which is of God, man becomes Godlike as in spirit, he is.

Therefore when he speaks, he speaks with the mouth of God. He speaks in truth; he speaks in love; and he speaks with authority, spiritually so, and there is no fear to be entertained. When man of Earth receives inspiration, he quite often expresses himself so, "I do not know why I think this..." He has received his great inspiration, even when he cannot account for it, as to why he so thinks, or why his deep conviction. We are speaking of that which is constructive, you understand, then worry not, nor become weary in well doing. Spiritual power is a tangible power which cannot be destroyed.

We desire, please, to have the truth of the Living God, not a living God, for there is but one God, the Living God, to be shared man to man, as brother to brother.

As you, dear ones, and all mankind of Earth express themselves, there is yet time, for we, of the Council, to give expression to truth, which shall emancipate man from the darkness of superstitious teachings.

When the seed is planted in fertile soil, it has abundant fruition, does it not? And the power which man calls God seeks to plant seeds in fertile soil.

There are many highways and byways where the message of truth must be given and where the barnacles of error and deception have fallen away into the depth of oblivion, and peace and harmony are being established. The sea that was rough is now becoming calm and peaceful. All this is being accomplished through messages of truth and love.

To those who have dedicated themselves to that great immutable principle of life, which God so ordained to be, there is no greater service than that of service to one's fellowman. Love is power. Love is light. Love is life.

A teacher of ancient age and one of the supreme teachers of the ancient mystical White Brotherhood, after the Order of Melchizedek, wishes to extend this message to you:

"This moment is very precious to us; the fields are rapidly ripening; we are in need of spiritual laborers in the field and in the vineyards. Our decision to call you to follow with us has not been a decision of a sudden moment, as you reckon time.

"You have been very well attended by subordinate members of our Council, and we find you now ready to answer the summons. We impose no task; you shall create the duty. We make no demands, for we are ever mindful that where distress, physically or otherwise, is evident, you shall consider it a sacred duty to share such understanding as you have gained, as it has benefited you, that it may benefit and help your brother.

169

"Do you ask me what is needful in your life, in your thinking, to surrender that you may serve with us? And I say with us, for we serve with one another. We make no demands of surrender. Should you find in your thinking such thoughts as govern your daily thinking and conduct, an obstruction to your service, we rest assured that you shall discard them. Such is our abiding faith with you, our confidence and our trust.

"We are not advocates of abolition, for it has become our experience that in due season, through reasoning and the desire to serve in a greater capacity, whatever shackles that may be binding will fall by the wayside. We rejoice with you, we rejoice with you.

"You are not leaving the mundane sphere of life, quite to the contrary. You are becoming a greater part of your fellowman than ever before. Whatever discrepancies may be revealed in your fellowman, you shall learn to bless. You shall lift the fallen and you shall lead those of unsteady, uncertain pace. The troubles of heart you shall learn to comfort, in the same manner that you have accepted comfort.

"Each service rendered shall bring you closer to the greater Eternal Cosmos of the universe, the Living God. Understanding shall be the cornerstone of your temple and upon that altar of your temple shall be the light of love, unfed by human hands. All of love which has been shared with you shall become magnified a thousand times ten thousand.

"Blessed are thou, blessed art thou among men of Earth. Blessed art thou, precious art thou. Ye have come forth from thy mother's womb precious in the sight of God. Blessed art thou.

"Thou shalt feed the sheep of the Father's pasture. Thou shalt take unto thy bosom the young lambs and thy voice shall sound as many laughing waters. Thou shalt gather the sweet grapes for the winepress. Thou shalt not drink of the bitter cup henceforth; the narrow of thy bones shall wax in richness.

"Blessed art thou, precious art thou. The yoke of the Father is light and chafeth not the heart. The will of the Father maketh no bearing of distress. Easy is the yoke, light the burden. Enter in, beloved.

"In the secret chamber of your soul's consciousness, you shall dedicate your honor. You are not bound by oath to man of Earth. You are not bound by oath to the Father of Fathers. Your yea shall be yea to truth, and your nay shall be nay to error, as thou deemest wise to live.

"Unto thee, I grant peace of mind. For he who hath peace of mind knoweth no troubled heart. He who loveth hath peace of mind.

"Think you not in strangeness of this visit. Man of Earth had made of me a brazen image, a molten idol! Thou art Christ's of God, as are all of the Father's house. Look not upon me as mighty or in greater measure than the humblest heart in God's universe. I come to you humble, contrite, your brother, your

171

friend, not ruler in tyranny creating strife. Not author of confusion, for we are authors of peace. So live with me, that I may so live with you. Bless you; bless you; bless you. A thousand times blessed are you.

"Unto thee, I grant thou shalt enter through faithfulness into the oneness of life, where thou shalt consume further desire to ever again tenant another physical body. This unto thee I grant, so shall it ever be. As a hen covereth her young, come unto my breast, in the fullness of the Father's house. It is finished."

You, dear ones, have conformed to the law of man that you may render a service to God and your fellowman. What can hinder you? Naught but your desire to forsake that unto which you have espoused yourself.

He who remains steadfast is God's ambassador. Disquieting hours come to man, but because of disquieting thoughts, it cannot be otherwise. There shall be no disquieting thought among you. The manner in which you give of your service, and the cause unto which you have espoused, shall express love of God. There may come moments when you, dear ones, shall meet with criticism, only on the part of those who do not understand. The reason that they do not care to understand is because of the infancy of their soul growth, for we are reading the record of their unfinished scroll of life. Bless you; bless you.

CHAPTER THIRTEEN

AN ANCIENT ONE SPEAKS

Greetings, sons and daughters of Lux.

Ages before the first stone was laid in the foundation of Solomon's Temple, you were builders, O sons and daughters of Lux. It is for that reason and none other that you have been guided and guarded from one embodiment to another so that in this hour, you shall build a greater temple than that of Solomon.

Builders are needed; craftsmen of the Living God, architects of the living, undying, Principle of Life. You shall only fail should you become confused with the carnal ideas of mortal man, and that we zealously guard against.

173

We have undertaken to lead you, step by step. You are never commanded to serve. Love inspires you; love is unselfish, and any man or woman in physical embodiment who learns to tread the unselfish path, travels the path of God.

We are now assembling the pillars of the new temple, O sons and daughters of light, the original Essenes, the master masons, builders.

Your faith in God, first and foremost, shall never permit the selfish arrows of mortal man to ever penetrate your hearts. These arrows emanate from the mortal thinking and are sent forth from man's bow of selfish persecution. As you have faith in God in one measure, you shall have faith in God in all measures.

When the confusion of mortal thinking crosses your path, in the stillness of your soul's consciousness, you shall say, "I am no part of you, for I am a daughter of light; I am a son of light."

You shall be like Buddha; you shall not accept the unrighteous act or gift. You shall be like the humble Galilean; you shall also say, "Get thee behind me, O thou evil." Also, as Buddha and as the Galilean, you shall behold and bless the Christ light of God in the consciousness of the one who would disturb the peace and quiet of your soul.

Remember, likewise, the words of the Nazarene, the chief elder teacher of the ancient mystical White Brotherhood, after the Order of Melchizedek, when he said, "I send you forth among wolves in sheep's clothing."

Ever be firm in truth, steadfast in your faith and understanding in God. Thus you shall remove the sheep's wool from the ravening wolves and you shall make of the wolves, lambs. The lambs shall grow into sturdy healthy sheep of the Father's pasture.

O sons and daughters of Lux, unto thee I grant this. So be it.

INDEX

FELLOW STUDENT:

The following index is offered to help the topical researcher. However, to make a truly complete index in all senses would be very tedious. Subjects such as God, love, truth and many others appear on practically every page, as the subjects and contexts are so interwoven. We have tried to pick the most important references.

179

184